4x4 travel guide
EASTERN AFRICA

Maureen Day

First published by Maureen Day in 2014 as *Beware of Falling Mangoes*
Second revised edition published by Maureen Day in 2016 as *4x4 Travel Guide Eastern Africa*

5 Green Acres, 42 Morcom Road, Prestbury, Pietermaritzburg, 3201
KwaZulu-Natal, South Africa
Cell: +27 (0) 766332757

Cover, Layout, Design and Mapwork: Marise and Candy Bauer, M Design

Photography: Maureen Day, with contributions from
Willy and Ingrid Hardman and Dave and Beryl Kotze.

Distributed by Penguin Random House South Africa (Pty) Ltd,
Reg. No. 1953/000441/07
The Estuaries No. 4, Oxbow Crescent (off Century Avenue), Century City, 7441, South Africa
P. O. Box 1144, Cape Town, 8000, South Africa
www.randomstruik.co.za

Printed and Bound in China by Leo Paper Products Ltd.

ISBN: 978-0-620-67051-7

DEDICATION
In Loving Memory of Lorraine Karg

'Until the next adventure …'

Lord, goodness is stronger than evil;
Love is stronger than hate;
Light is stronger than darkness;
Life is stronger than death;
Victory is ours through you who love us.

Amen.

– Archbishop emeritus Desmond Tutu

THANK YOU

To the people of Africa who invited us into their lives, for their help, generosity and friendship too. Without them, our adventure would not have been as memorable.

To my parents, Bob and Denise McLelland and to Carl Botha, for watching over our home and pets.

To Willy and Ingrid Hardman and Dave and Beryl Kotze for the use of their photographs.

Last but not least: our many friends who so generously gave of their time and experience, love and support.

UMGUNGUNDLOVU TO AKSUM
Willy, Ingrid, Beryl, Dave, Brian, Maureen, Neville and Lorraine

CONTENTS

3 — AN AFRICAN BLESSING

5 — IN THE BEGINNING

Travel Companions 6
Choosing a Campsite 6
Rules of the Road 7
Compiling an Itinerary 8

11 — SUPPLIES

Documentation Required 12
Vehicle Requirements 14
Cab Requirements 17
Medical 19
Equipment 23
Kitchen Utensils 25
Grocery List 26
Bush Recipes 28
Clothing and Toiletries 32
Planning on the Home Front 34

37 — ROUTE PLANNING

Our Journey through eastern Africa 38
Zambia 46
Malawi 62
Tanzania 70
Uganda 94
Kenya 118
Ethiopia 158

197 — WITH HINDSIGHT

200 — INDEX

AN AFRICAN BLESSING

May the African sun always shine on you
May the rhythm of its drums beat deeply in your heart
May the vision of its glory fill you with joy
And may the memory of Africa be with you always

IN THE BEGINNING

1 Travel Companions

2 Choosing a Campsite

3 Rules of the Road

4 Compiling an Itinerary

■ Travel Companions

- Choose companions you know well and socialise with on a regular basis.
- Ensure there are no personal agendas that will have a disruptive impact on the group at a later stage.
- Avoid taking on last-minute newcomers whom you do not know. This could lead to personality clashes among members of the group, causing a divide and an unpleasant atmosphere.

■ Choosing a Campsite

- Choose level ground preferably with lots of green grass and shade.
- Check the grass for safari ants.
- Don't set up camp on or near a game path.
- Check for dead branches overhead.
- Make sure that the tree you have chosen to camp under is not used by a troop of baboons to roost in at night.
- Which direction is the wind coming from?
- Avoid potential noise from fellow travelers, generators, pubs or main roads.
- Be aware of potential threats to your safety or security.
- Respect the environment. Keep noise levels to a minimum. Take your garbage with you. Make sure the campfire has been extinguished.
- Never camp in dry riverbeds. Flash floods are a real danger.

IN THE BEGINNING

Queen Elizabeth National Park, Uganda

■ Rules of the Road

Now what?

- Fill up when fuel is available.
- Draw funds when you pass an ATM or bank.
- The slowest vehicle sets the pace.
- The vehicle in front is responsible for the vehicle behind.
- The members of each vehicle are responsible for bringing their own maps; and should also contribute to the day's travel decisions.
- Where possible, try not to do more than 300 kilometres a day.
- Take regular breaks to top up on sustenance, relieve fatigue and check on the vehicle.
- Mechanical problems should be fixed as soon as possible to avoid placing the group at risk and to prevent further problems down the road.

THE ZAMBEZI RIVER

The Zambezi River is 2 700 kilometres long and flows through 6 countries. It is the fourth longest river in Africa.

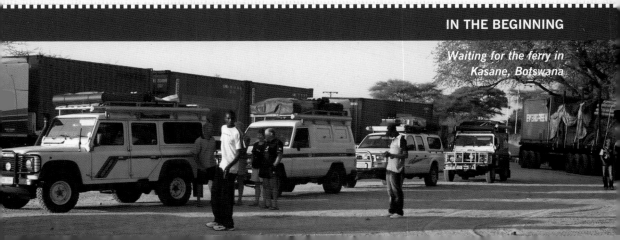

IN THE BEGINNING

Waiting for the ferry in Kasane, Botswana

■ Compiling an Itinerary

Malachite Kingfisher

An itinerary is important in that it ensures you do not run out of money halfway through the trip, drive past places of interest or waste expensive fuel driving all over the place. Here are some tips to get you going:

1. The research into each country is a huge task that each member of the group should be involved in.

2. Determine who likes to do what so that everyone's needs are met. For example, bird watching, game viewing, hiking etc.

3. Give careful consideration to road conditions, distances, GPS coordinates, fuel availability and projected daily expenses.

4. Determine if towns en route offer banking facilities, vehicle repairs, supermarkets and accommodation. You might just have to make an unexpected stop.

5. Note down all items of interest en route and costs involved to visit.

IN THE BEGINNING

- Check everyone's passport before departing from the border post to ensure that everyone has the same entry stamps and number of days allocated to visit.
- Land Rover and Land Cruiser spares are available throughout eastern Africa.

6. Have several accommodation options for the night. What looks good in travel books is not necessarily the case. Decide how long you would like to stay.

7. Under a general category, note the following on each country:

    *   Contact details of foreign embassies whose assistance you may require.
    *   What visas need to be purchased in advance, costs involved and where to apply for extensions.
    *   Public holidays.
    *   Road rules and vehicle requirements – www.aa.co.za.
    *   Emergency service telephone numbers, area codes and directory assistance.
    *   ATM availability, banks and foreign exchange outlets.
    *   Check embassy websites for warnings, scams, possible location of landmines, policies on the taking of photographs, etc.
    *   Airline offices and contact details.
    *   Medical facilities.

8. Enter all coordinates into your GPS in advance.

9. Include photocopies of maps that show the layout of local towns, how to get in and around game reserves, etc. The more information, the better.

10. Add up the costs involved to get an estimate of the financial requirements for the trip. Don't forget to allocate funds for your return home!

Most drivers north of our border do not possess emergency triangles or just don't bother to use them. Instead they use branches from a tree or a row of rocks across the road to alert traffic to a potential problem up ahead.

IN THE BEGINNING

SATELLITE PHONE

A satellite phone is a mobile phone that sends and receives calls using satellites rather than landlines or cellular broadcasting towers. The phone only requires a clear line of sight to the sky, so calls can be made from any location. The disadvantage of a satellite phone is the noticeable delay in conversations, as the signal travels to the satellite and on to the sender or receiver. Satellite minutes are also more expensive than cellular minutes. View the following sites for additional information: www.satcomms.co.za, www.ashburysatcom.co.za and www.rentasat.co.za.

SUPPLIES

1. Documentation Required
2. Vehicle Requirements
3. Cab Requirements
4. Medical
5. Equipment
6. Kitchen Utensils
7. Grocery List
8. Bush Recipes
9. Clothing and Toiletries
10. Planning on the Home Front

■ Documentation Required

- Passport – valid for at least six months after you plan to use it.

- Identity document.

- Driver's license and an AA-recognised International Driver's License (IDL) – check the expiry date.

- Vaccination card.

- Vehicle clearance from the Vehicle Identification and Safeguarding Unit of the SAP.

- Certificate of registration for the vehicle.

- Letter of permission from the bank to (a) take the vehicle out of the country or (b) provide proof of ownership.

- A doctor's prescription for personal medication.

- Carnet de Passage (see page 13).

- Comesa Yellow Card (see page 13).

- Vehicle insurance.

- Medical aid cover.

- A list of all medical supplies on board.

- Make, model, serial number and engine number of the vehicle, boat and trailer.

- Make, model and serial number of the radio, camera, video, fridge and freezer too. Keep this information together with your passport number, date and place of issue and date of expiry, on a separate laminated sheet for easy use at the border post.

SUPPLIES

- Photocopy at least two copies of the above documentation, including visas. Additional copies can be made en route if required.
- Give one copy to a fellow traveller, with your spare vehicle keys and next of kin details.
- Have all photocopies verified on the same side of the page as the photocopy.

Carnet de Passage

The Carnet de Passage is a form of insurance that protects you from import duties should anything happen to your vehicle whilst in a foreign country. It also eases your passage through border posts. Visit www.aa.co.za for further information, costs involved, requirements and an application form. Otherwise contact the nearest branch of the Automobile Association or call the South African foreign travel department on telephone number +27 (0) 11 7991040.

Comesa Yellow Card

The Comesa Yellow Card is an extension of your third-party insurance cover, to include foreign countries who are Comesa members. The card can be purchased from insurance companies in any of the participating member states.

ZSIC, Premium House, 4432 Independence Avenue, Lusaka, Zambia
Cell: +260 (0) 977849283 – Mavis Ndumba
E-mail: cmpandamwike@zsicgi.co.za

Business hours are from 08:00 to 17:00 weekdays and 09:00 to 13:00 on Saturday.

Vehicle Insurance – Cross Country

Vehicle insurance on any trip through Africa is very important. To ensure peace of mind and excellent care, we recommend Cross Country. The service we received was excellent; our vehicle needs were met and as a result we made it home in one piece with some truly amazing memories.

Thank you, Cross Country, for a job well done.

South Africa – Tel: +27 (0) 11 2158800
E-mail: info@ccic.co.za
Web: www.ccic.co.za

SUPPLIES

- Keep all documents together in a waterproof bag.
- Include five passport photographs per passport holder.
- Check expiry dates on all relevant documents.
- Obtain a letter of reference from the South African embassy for those countries further north who may require one.

■ Vehicle Requirements

When one takes into consideration the condition of some of Africa's roads and the vast distances between civilisation and a spares shop, it makes common sense to prepare thoroughly before any major trip.

Although the following list of spares/ requirements seems a little over the top, it is simply a list of what you may require depending on the route you plan to follow. To lighten the load, you may wish to share spares with a fellow traveller, provided you stick together for the duration of the trip.

Accessories

- A 6 amp solar panel
- Battery charger for three auxillary Deltic batteries
- Electronic temperature gauge for reading the engine block temperature
- Emu Suspension and bushes with double rear shocks to correct swaying
- Enlargement of the radiator for improved cooling
- Fire extinguisher

- Fitted skid plate to protect the sump and steering arm
- Float switch in the radiator reserve water bottle to determine water level
- Four batteries (three auxillary)
- Galvanised wrap around bull bar with winch
- Grass screen and hook
- Inverter to run the angle grinder and drill, for charging batteries, GPS, camera, video and computer
- Removable windscreen cable protectors
- Roll bar
- Shade cloth to lie on
- Snorkel
- Stickers to identify diesel and water ports
- Two-way radios
- Winch control box cover
- Window reinforcement with Smash and Grab (a protective barrier on windows)
- Wire

Camping

- Scotch Guard the rooftop tent
- Silicon spray for zips

SUPPLIES

- When purchasing foreign currency, be sure to take your passport, vehicle registration and utility bill as proof of residence.
- Should you be unable to drive your vehicle, you are required by law to state in writing, that the driver of the vehicle has your permission to drive it on your behalf.
- Check the vehicle license expiry date.

Electrical

- Alternator
- Assorted fuses
- Assorted electrical wire and connectors
- Assorted spare globes

General Spares

- Anti-freeze
- Assorted nuts and bolts
- Brake pads and pins
- Cable ties – assorted
- Cambelt
- Duct tape
- Fan belts
- Insulation tape
- Pratley's Putty and Pratley's quick set glue
- Prop shaft universal joints
- Q20
- Radiator cap
- Radiator hose and assorted clamps
- Rags and hand cleaner
- Remote control batteries
- Silicone for vehicle water leaks
- Tie rod ends
- Water pump
- Wheel bearings
- Windscreen cleaner

Lights

- Fitted spot and fog lights
- Headlight protectors

Recovery

- D-shackles (assorted sizes)
- Gloves
- Hi-Lift jack, bottle jack (two stage) and laminated wooden block
- Hi-Lift jacking points to avoid vehicle damage
- Kinetic strap
- Sand ladder or rubber conveyor belting for sand driving
- Snatch block
- Spade
- Tree trunk protector strap
- Tyre chains
- Winch

As a result of bad road conditions, the inner tube was frequently 'pinched', resulting in a total of 30 flat tyres on our vehicle!

SUPPLIES

Safety

- Reflective safety jacket/vest
- Two triangles

Service Kit

- Air filter
- Brake and clutch fluid
- Differential gear oil – for diff and transfer box
- Fuel filter
- Gearbox oil
- Oil filter
- Power steering fluid
- Sufficient engine oil for a service

EXCERPT FROM A LETTER SENT HOME

We then had to spend several days in Nairobi for vehicle repairs. The clutch had gone, one engine bracket was broken and the brakes were worn. The cracks in the windscreen frame needed to have support brackets inserted to stabilise the windscreen, and prevent further damage to the frame.

Tools

- Angle grinder
- Clear plastic siphon pipe
- Drill
- Long extension cord
- Rubber hammer
- Small grease gun
- Toolbox
- Welding glass
- Welding rods

Tyres

- A 12 volt tyre pump
- Fitted steel valve caps (plastic ones break)
- Pressure gauge and valve key for tyres with tubes
- Tube patches (assorted) and glue
- Tubeless plugs for tubeless tyres
- Two spare tyre tubes
- Two spare tyres with no rim
- Tyre lever

SUPPLIES

Stuck! Mt Elgon, Uganda

◼ Cab Requirements

- Address list for promised postcards
- Binoculars
- Bird and game books
- Booking references and receipts
- Calculator
- Car window guard: an adjustable grid used in car windows for pets. Ideal for security when vehicle windows are open
- Camera and video camera. When not in use, store in a pillow slip to protect from dust and dirt
- Cellular telephone and charger
- Contact details of rescue services
- Credit cards
- Documents
- Garbage bag
- GPS, charger and Tracks4Africa programme
- Hat or cap
- House keys
- Itinerary
- Lip Ice
- Maps

PACKING YOUR VEHICLE

No two vehicles are packed the same, but here are a few points to bear in mind:

1. Vehicle tools and spares, the first-aid box and fire extinguisher must be quick and easy to retrieve.

2. Take into consideration the fact that you may have to spend the odd night sleeping in your vehicle.

3. Distribute weight evenly.

4. In some places you may be required to transport a security guard or guide.

5. Secure everything. In the event of an accident, your belongings could kill you.

- Mosquito repellent and fly spray
- Music. Store CDs in a dust-free container with a CD cleaner
- Pain relief tablets

SUPPLIES

Major engine repairs, Uganda

En route to the Bangweulu Wetland, Zambia

- Paintbrush. Ideal for cleaning dust and dirt out of all the hard-to-reach places
- Pen and notebook
- Pepper spray
- Permits
- Photographs. Of home, family and pets
- Safe. Bolted to the vehicle in a secure, accessible place
- Satellite phone
- Snacks
- Spare remote control batteries
- Sunglasses
- Toilet roll
- Toll fees
- Torch
- Umbrella
- Wallet
- Water and water bottles
- Wet Wipes
- Ziplock bags for easy storage of border documents that may still be valid on your return. It is also a good idea to empty your wallet so that the currency from one country does not mix with another

SUPPLIES

Meat and dairy products are know carriers of disease, making it illegal to carry these products from one country to another. If found in your possession, border officials are legally bound to confiscate and destroy the items.

To call home at a cheaper rate, we used one of the many cellular networks available in eastern Africa. SIM cards can be purchased at supermarkets and an assortment of local shops.

Internet facilities are available in even the smallest of towns. Just ask around as they are often situated in the most amazing places.

ATMs are widely available throughout eastern Africa. A Visa Card gives greater accessibility to cash, and US dollars are preferred over the British pound.

Paying with US dollars can lead to some frustration as notes dated prior to 2003 and those depicting presidents with 'small heads' are turned away, as are amounts smaller than US$50.00 attract a far lower exchange rate. However, smaller notes do come in handy when faced with the 'I do not have any change' situation. Currency should be changed in the main cities, where possible, as rates elsewhere often amount to daylight robbery. If changing money at the border, beware of con men.

■ Medical

Medical Aid Cover

On investigation, we discovered that our local medical aid would not provide medical cover beyond our borders. That left us with two options: pay up or cancel. Unfortunately, in this day and age one cannot afford to be without medical cover, so we paid for a year's base line option and set about looking for a medical aid provider for the trip. We eventually settled for AIG Assist.

AIG Assist

South Africa – Tel: +27 (0) 11 5253109
E-mail: aigservices@internationalsos.com
Web: www.aig.co.za

Do not leave home without adequate medical insurance. AIG Assist offers excellent cover, with evacuation, if required.

SUPPLIES

SECURITY

Security is always a concern when travelling in foreign countries. You never know what you might have to deal with, especially in remote areas. As a precaution, the cab windows were reinforced with smash and grab and steel mesh was placed on the windows at the back of the cab. We also carried a catapult for troublesome baboons, a sjambok and pepper spray. No compromising situation was encountered, but better be safe than sorry.

As an added precaution, each vehicle had a comprehensive first-aid box containing the following:

- Airway
- Antacids – Rennies or Gavascon
- Anti-inflammatory gel
- Antiemetics – Nauzine or Stemitil tablets
- Antifungal cream
- Antihistamine cream
- Antiseptic
- Asthma pump
- Burn seal
- Cervical collar
- Cloves for toothache
- Coartem
- Cotton wool
- Crepe and triangular bandages with clips
- D-Worm
- Disposable gloves
- Elastoplast/plasters
- Emergency blanket
- Eye pad
- Eye ointment/drops

- Flu remedy and multivitamins
- General antibiotic tablets and cream
- Hydrocortisone cream
- Imodium tablets
- Jellonet
- Laxatives
- Lignocaine
- Malaria tablets and test kit
- Micropore tape
- Mosquito repellent
- Opsite
- Pain relief tablets
- Prescription medication
- Rehydrate. Otherwise dissolve eight teaspoons of sugar and half a teaspoon of salt into one litre of water
- Safety pins
- Scissors
- Sleeping pills
- Spare pair of prescription glasses
- Splints
- Steri-Strips

SUPPLIES

- If you are planning to be away over the New Year, delegate a responsible person to submit your medical aid choice of cover on your behalf.
- Spray the inside of the cab in the morning to get rid of mosquitoes that gained entry during the night.

- Sterile dressing packs. We made our own drapes and with some cotton wool balls, gauze and gloves we took them down to the local hospital and had them sterilised
- Stitch cutters
- Strepsils
- Sutures – 4.0 nylon
- Syringes, needles and sterile wipes (assorted)
- Thermometer
- Tweezers
- Water purification tablets
- 18 to 21 gauge needles, giving sets, 1L Ringer's Lactate and 1L Sodium Chloride. Although you may not know how to erect a drip, the bush clinics throughout Africa are very experienced but lack the equipment.
- Pethidine/Stemitil ampoules. You will need a doctor's prescription for this one but it's well worth the effort. In Ethiopia I had a bad bout of diarrhoea and vomiting (caused by unpasteurised milk in a cappuccino) and couldn't keep the tablets down long enough to get it under control. Without the Stemitil this scenario could have been a lot worse.

Doxycycline tablets were used for the prevention of malaria. However, several members of the group developed an assortment of reactions to the drug. These included skin discoloration, bleeding under the nails, thrush, painful skin eruptions, bad dreams and hallucinations! The drug was immediately discontinued and we purchased extra Coartem tablets as a precaution. I am happy to say that no one got malaria!

Vaccinations

Vaccinations need to be administered eight to six months prior to departure and must be recorded on the International Certificate of Vaccination card. Here is a list of the basic vaccinations required:

- Meningitis
- Polio
- Tetanus
- Twinrix (Hepatitis A and B)
- Typhoid
- Yellow Fever

SUPPLIES

VEHICLE SIGNAGE

Vehicle signage plays an important role in communication and its value should not be underestimated. We applied several stickers to the Land Rover, including the South African flag, Mandela and several Zulu words of greeting. With hindsight, we should also have included Bafana Bafana! It wasn't long before we realised the importance of these stickers as the local people came forward to shake our hands, ask a million questions and jump up and down with excitement!

Diseases have a way of popping up all over Africa at the most inopportune moments, so it would be advisable to check with your doctor or local travel clinic for any additional vaccinations you may require.

> Vaccinations recorded on the vaccination card may not mean much to a grumpy border official looking for an excuse to make your life a misery. For example: Twinrix.
>
> It would be advisable to ask medical personnel to be specific when recording vaccinations given. For example: Twinrix (Hepatitis A and B). I would also suggest that you keep the package insert as proof of what the Twinrix vaccination is for.

Medical Tips

- Keep all medication in a sealed container and in a cool dark spot.
- Keep a first-aid book for reference.
- Compile a brief medical history. Be sure to include any known allergies, your blood group, any medication you may be taking, previous operations and any adverse reaction to anaesthetic. Also note the contact details of your doctor and medical aid. Keep a copy on hand and give a copy to members of the group.
- Purchase cheap 'dog tags' and have them engraved with the following information: name, passport number, blood group, allergies, medication and contact details of your doctor and medical aid. You never know when you may not be able to speak for yourself.
- Have a full medical and dental check-up prior to departure.
- It is vital that every member in the group knows how to perform CPR and the Heimlich manoeuvre.
- Bottled water is available at a reasonable price throughout eastern Africa. Make sure the top is secure before purchasing.
- Compile a list of emergency telephone numbers, including that of family, friends and anyone else who may be able to help at a time of crisis.
- Pile cream is excellent for taking the sting out of tsetse fly bites!

SUPPLIES

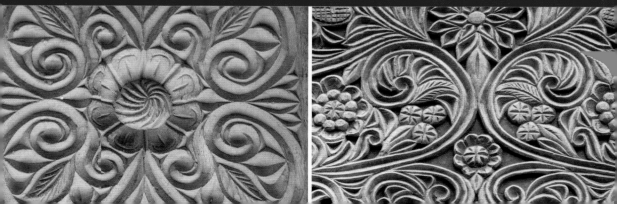

■ Equipment

- Adaptor
- Ammo boxes with spare clips
- Assorted containers for leftover food
- Axe
- Backpack
- Bags – shopping
- Batteries
- Binoculars
- Blankets
- Books – guide, travel and reading
- Bow saw and blade
- Braai grid and tongs
- Brush and pan
- Bucket for water
- Camera, charger, memory card, CDs, bag and batteries
- Catty
- Chairs
- Charcoal
- Clippers – garden
- Cooking pots and pans
- Firelighters
- Fishing rod

- Fitted and top sheet
- Fly swatter
- Fridge and freezer
- Frying pan
- Gas bottle cover
- Gas bottle grub plugs, washer seals, jets, key and O-rings
- Gas mantle
- Gas – small portable *
- Gas stove and regulator
- GPS and charger
- Groundsheet *
- Headlamp
- Hot-water bottles
- Laces – boot *
- Lapa *
- Leatherman
- Life jackets, mask, snorkel and fins
- Matches or lighter
- Mattress cover
- Mattress – ground *
- Mirror
- Mosquito net
- Padlocks
- Pegs and nylon rope for a washing line

- Pens, pencils, writing paper, envelopes and notebook
- Pepper spray
- Pillows
- Plastic potty
- Playing cards
- Plugs to recharge electrical gear
- Rat trap
- Sewing kit *
- Shade cloth *
- Shower bag – solar
- Shower cubicle *
- Sleeping bag sheets *
- Sleeping bags or duvet*
- Spare sink plug
- Spotlight and charger
- String *
- Tent *
- Tent pegs
- Toilet
- Torch, globes and batteries

- Umbrella
- Video and tapes
- Sputnick washing machine
- Water bottles
- Waterproof bag

* Denotes items taken but not used.

In most instances, when away from the vehicle for several days, it worked out cheaper to deal with an agent and purchase a package tour that included accommodation and meals, especially to Zanzibar and Lamu Islands. As a result, we didn't need certain equipment we had brought with us.

From Tanzania northwards, the Cadac gas bottle refill nozzle does not fit its counterpart. If you purchase a bottle of gas locally, be sure to check that it fits onto your equipment.

Brian fishing on Lake Victoria, Uganda

■ Kitchen Utensils

- Basin for dishes
- Bin bags
- Bottle opener
- Bread knife
- Breadboard
- Can opener
- Cereal bowl
- Cooker
- Cooking pots
- Dinner plates
- Dish towels and cloths
- Dishwashing liquid
- Drying rack
- Egg cups
- Egg lifter
- Food umbrella
- Frying pan
- Foil
- Grater
- Hand towels
- Herb containers
- Kettle
- Knives, forks, spoons and teaspoons
- Ice blocks
- Ice cube trays

- Jelly tubs
- Jug
- Lighter and matches
- Masking tape (to seal packets)
- Measuring spoons
- Measuring jug
- Mugs
- Potato peeler
- Pot scourer
- Potjie pot and stand
- Salad bowl
- Scissors
- Scrubbing brush
- Serving spoons
- Side plates
- Sieve
- Table
- Tablecloth
- Toaster
- Toothpicks
- Tupperware shaker
- Vegetable knife
- Water container
- Water/juice bottles
- Whisk
- Wooden spoon
- Ziplock bags

SUPPLIES

LDC

This is a marvellous product – and I never leave home without it! LDC is a concentrated, earth friendly, multi-purpose light duty cleaner that comes in a 1 or 5 litre leak-proof container. As a dishwashing liquid, it removes grease in cold water, saving valuable gas. As a body soap, it doesn't dry your skin like commercial soaps. As a clothes washing liquid, it will not damage your clothes or irritate your skin, should there be insufficient water to rinse. As a de-greaser, it will even remove engine oil! For more information, contact Ann-Rose Oldham (GNLD ID 26976056) on aroldham@telkomsa.net.

■ Grocery List

- Apples, bananas and oranges
- Asparagus – tinned
- Assorted dried fruit
- Assorted snacks for the cab
- Bacon
- Baked Beans – tinned
- Mixed Beans – tinned
- Beer
- Bin bags
- Biscuits – savoury and sweet
- Bovril
- Braai pack
- Bread. Place a few slices in a Ziplock bag and pop them in the freezer
- Butter
- Butter beans – tinned
- Butternut
- Cereals
- Chakalaka – tinned
- Cheese – grated
- Cheese wedges
- Chewing gum
- Chicken portions
- Chips
- Chops
- Chutney
- Coffee
- Cool drinks
- Curry powder
- Custard
- Eggs
- Energy bars
- Fillet
- Fish – frozen or curried in a tin
- Fish spice
- Flour and baking powder
- Foil
- Fruit – assorted in tins
- Garlic
- Gem squash
- Gherkins
- Gravy
- Haddock
- Ham – tinned
- Herbs – assorted
- Honey
- Jam – assorted
- Jelly
- Juice – powdered, eg. Game
- Kebab sticks
- Kippers – tinned
- Lemon juice
- Lentils

SUPPLIES

- If you are planning to be away from your vehicle for any length of time, bear in mind the need for light, easy-to-carry cooking utensils.
- Drinking yoghurt bottles (200 ml) are ideal as juice bottles. They don't leak or take up too much space in the fridge.
- When buying avocado pears, make sure the pip inside is not loose, or the inside of the fruit will bruise every time you hit a bump in the road.
- Pre-cook dinner for the first couple of nights.

- Macaroni
- Marshmallows
- Milk – condensed
- Milk – long-life
- Milk – powdered
- Mincemeat
- Muffin mix
- Mushrooms – tinned
- Mussels – tinned
- Mustard
- Nuts – assorted
- Oats
- Olive oil
- Olives
- Onions
- Paper plates
- Pasta sauce
- Peanut butter
- Peanuts
- Peas – frozen or tinned
- Pilchards – tinned
- Pineapple
- Popcorn
- Potatoes
- Pumpkin
- Recipe ingredients
- Rice
- Roller towel

- Rusks
- Salad dressing
- Salads – boxed
- Salami
- Salt and pepper
- Sardines – tinned
- Sausage
- Smash (instant potato)
- Soup in a packet
- Spaghetti
- Spray and Cook
- Stock cubes
- Sugar
- Sweetcorn – tinned
- Sweets
- Tabasco
- Tea
- Toilet rolls
- Tomato puree
- Tomato sauce
- Tomatoes
- Tomatoes – tinned
- Tuna in a packet
- Vitamins and minerals
- Washing powder and Sunlight soap
- Weet-Bix
- Wine

SUPPLIES

- Cut a block of butter into cubes, wrap in foil and freeze. Use one small block at a time.
- For easy identification of tin contents, once packed, write the details on the lid of the tin.
- Number ammo boxes and list everything in each box for quick retrieval.
- Use a flat-bottomed potjie pot if planning to bake bread and muffins.
- Pre-pack meat into Ziplock bags, which can be reused for meat purchases along the way.
- Grate cheddar cheese, pack into small bags, and freeze for sandwiches and macaroni.

■ Bush Recipes

Marinade

- 2 tablespoons of brown sugar
- 1 tablespoon of Worcestershire sauce
- 2 tablespoons of lemon juice
- Pinch of salt

Pineapple Chicken

- 4 chicken pieces
- 4 tablespoons of oil
- 1 green pepper, chopped
- 2 celery stalks, chopped
- 1 onion, chopped
- 198g of pineapple slices – keep the juice
- 1 tablespoon each of soy sauce, lemon juice and tomato puree
- Seasoning

1. Fry chicken until brown.
2. Add green pepper, celery and onion – sauté.
3. Add pineapple juice, soy sauce, lemon juice, tomato puree and seasoning.
4. Simmer for 30 minutes until cooked.
5. Arrange pineapple slices on top of the chicken pieces. Heat for 5 minutes. Serve with rice.

Tennis Biscuit Pudding

- 2 packets of Tennis biscuits
- ½ a cup of lemon juice
- 1 tin condensed milk (199g)
- 825ml cool custard

1. Line oblong dish with whole Tennis biscuits.
2. Beat condensed milk and lemon juice until thick and creamy. Pour over the biscuits.
3. Add another layer of biscuits and cover with custard.
4. Chill for about 2 hours before serving.

Broccoli Salad

- 2 bunches raw broccoli, chopped
- 1 onion, chopped
- 2 cups grated cheese
- Bacon, cooked and chopped

Pilchard Salad

- 1 tin of pilchards, mashed
- 1 onion, chopped
- 1 tomato, chopped
- 1 green pepper, chopped
- Cooked rice

SUPPLIES

- If you can cook it, boil it or peel it, you can eat it...otherwise forget it.
- Beware of ice cream that might have melted and refrozen.
- Avoid drinking tap water – in ice form too.

Fruit and vegetables from roadside stalls

Curried Rice

- 1 large onion finely chopped
- 12,5ml butter – not margarine
- 250ml uncooked rice
- 500ml hot water
- 1 beef stock cube
- 50ml seedless raisins
- 2ml curry powder

1. Fry onion in the butter until soft.
2. Dissolve beef stock cube in 500ml of hot water.
3. Mix all ingredients together in an ovenproof dish, cover and bake at 180° for approximately 30 minutes.
4. This dish can be cooked in the potjie pot with hot coals placed under the potjie pot and on the lid.

Sweetcorn Fritters

- 410g can of creamed sweetcorn
- 1 egg, beaten
- Seasoning and parsley
- 1 onion finely chopped
- Garlic
- 1 cup self-raising flour
- Oil to fry

1. Mix ingredients.
2. Form the mixture into patties and fry until golden brown on both sides.
3. Delicious for breakfast with golden syrup.
4. Fried bacon or cooked ham, chopped into pieces, may also be added.

Hunter's Dish

- 2 onions, chopped
- 50g butter
- 225g mincemeat
- 300ml stock – 1½ stock cubes dissolved in 300ml of hot water
- 3 cloves
- Seasoning, bay leaves and curry powder
- 1 apple peeled and chopped
- 450g mashed potato
- 15g butter
- Fresh breadcrumbs

1. Fry the onions in butter until soft.
2. Add the remaining ingredients except the breadcrumbs and butter.
3. Simmer for half an hour.
4. Pour into a greased ovenproof dish.
5. Sprinkle breadcrumbs on top.

SUPPLIES

Northern Kenya

DID YOU KNOW?

The word 'safari' is derived from the Arab word 'safar' and is Swahili for 'expedition or traveller's caravan.'

6. Dot with butter and brown in a hot oven.
7. This dish can be cooked in the potjie pot. Once the breadcrumbs have been added, turn the lid of the potjie pot upside down and place hot coals on the lid. This will brown the breadcrumbs.

Potato Cakes (4)

- 1 packet instant potato
- 1 egg
- Seasoning
- Bacon, fried and cut into small pieces
- 1 grated onion
- Egg and breadcrumbs for coating
- Oil to fry

1. Mix the potato with water and allow to cool.
2. Add the remaining ingredients to the potato.
3. Mix well and form into patties.
4. Coat with egg and breadcrumbs.
5. Fry until golden brown.

Apple/Pear Crumble

- 2½ cups of cake flour
- 1 small cup of sugar – not too much or the pie will be very sweet
- ½ cup of margarine or butter
- 385g tin of unsweetened sliced pie apples.

1. Drain juice from the apple slices.
2. Place the apple slices in an ovenproof dish. Cut into smaller pieces.
3. Place the flour in a bowl. Add the butter, and with your fingers work the butter into the flour until it looks like breadcrumbs. Add a little sugar.
4. Sprinkle evenly on top of the apple slices.
5. Sprinkle sugar and cinnamon on top and bake for approximately 45 minutes.

I baked this dish in a normal pot with the lid turned over and coals on top.

Need a cup of buttermilk?

Try 1 tablespoon of vinegar/lemon juice in one cup of milk. Let it stand for 5 minutes.

Need a cup of honey?

Mix ¾ cup of sugar with ¼ cup of water.

SUPPLIES

Curried Apricot Chicken

Mix a large spoonful of apricot jam and curry powder with a cup of chicken stock. Toss chicken pieces and soft dried apricots into the mixture, and bake on a hot fire for 20–25 minutes until cooked through.

Buttermilk Bread

- 500g self-raising flour
- 500ml of buttermilk
- 1 packet clear onion soup

1. Place the flour and dry onion soup in a bowl – leave a little flour over to knead the dough.
2. Gradually add the buttermilk to form a sticky dough. I find there is invariably some buttermilk left over.
3. Sprinkle some flour on a flat surface and knead the dough.
4. Place the dough in a flat-bottomed potjie pot.
5. Place the potjie pot on a triangular stand with hot coals under the pot and all over the lid.
6. Cook for 45 minutes. Be careful not to get ash from the coal onto the bread when checking to see if it is cooked.

Tuna Cakes

- 2 170g cans of shredded tuna – drained
- 2 potatoes, peeled, cut into chunks and boiled until soft
- 1 small onion finely chopped
- 2 eggs lightly beaten
- Seasoning
- Oil to fry

1. Mash cooked potatoes.
2. Mix in tuna, egg, onion and seasoning.
3. Form into patties.
4. Fry in hot oil until golden brown.

■ Clothing and Toiletries

Toiletries

- Body lotion
- Contact lens cleaner
- Dental floss
- Deodorant
- Ear buds
- Face cloth
- Face cream
- Face wash
- Hair brush
- Hair clippers
- Lip Ice
- Mirror
- Nail clippers
- Razor and blades
- Sanitary pads/tampons and contraception

- Scrubbing brush
- Shampoo and conditioner
- Slip-slops for showering
- Soap
- Sunblock
- Tissues
- Toilet roll
- Toothbrush and toothpaste
- Towels
- Wash bags
- Wet Wipes

Clothing – Hers

- Alarm
- Backpack
- Beanie, gloves and scarf – it gets very cold in some parts of Ethiopia!
- Boots
- Gumboots
- Hat
- Jacket
- Jersey
- Light waterproof jacket
- Raincoat
- Sarongs
- Shoe bags
- Shorts

- Sleepwear
- Socks
- Strops
- Swimming costume
- Tracksuit
- Trousers
- T-shirts
- Underwear

Clothing – His

- Beanie, scarf and gloves
- Boots
- Gumboots
- Jacket
- Jersey
- Light waterproof jacket
- Raincoat
- Shoe bags
- Shorts
- Socks
- Strops
- Swimming costume
- Tracksuit
- Trousers
- T-shirts
- Underpants

TIPS

- With the exception of beauty products, we were able to replace toiletries throughout eastern Africa.

- Use hand towels instead of bath towels. They are easier to wash, don't take up much space and dry quickly.

- Purchase towels in a dark colour. It hides the dirt!

- Carry a packet of tissues in your pocket in case nature makes an unexpected call.

- Disposable underwear comes in handy if water is at a minimum.

- Purchase clothing that does not crease easily and that will dry overnight.

- To keep underwear free of dust, pop it into a Ziplock bag.

If you think you are too small to make a difference, you haven't spent a night with a mosquito!

■ Planning on the Home Front

Unfortunately, you cannot pack your bags and head for the wild plains of Africa without first taking care of your home. The following list should help to ensure that nothing is left to chance:

- Power of attorney to a responsible family member
- Mortgage payments
- Pension payments
- Medical Aid. Payment versus cancellation
- Bank account fees or cancellation
- Additional vehicles – payment, license renewal, insurance and storage
- Cancellation of telephone, cellular phone and Internet connection
- Monthly payment of water, electricity and rates
- Home insurance
- Set timers on light switches
- Cancellation of magazine subscriptions, club/gym membership and newspaper
- Update wills
- Pets – monies available for food and possible veterinarian bills, vaccinations, ID tags and collars on, clinic cards, leads, brushes, toys, bedding, medication, flea drops, food, water bowls, deworming tablets and medication for thunder/fireworks
- Domestic worker/gardener – UIF, letter of reference, monthly wages and leave owing, tea and lunch, toilet rolls, cleaning materials, emergency telephone numbers, list of chores and cellular phone airtime in case of an emergency
- Garden service – cancellation, access to the property, monthly payments, supervision, list of chores and refuse removal
- Fire extinguishers checked
- Television license and DSTV payments
- Alarm payments and change in contact telephone numbers
- Tax returns/extension

SUPPLIES

- Jewellery, will and gun into safe keeping
- Place indoor plants with a friend
- Switch off unused plug points
- Switch off the geyser
- Shut off the water mains

The House Sitter

In order to look after your home effectively, the house sitter will require a comprehensive handover on the day-to-day workings of your home. Here are some suggestions:

- Rental agreement
- A remote control for the electric gate
- A set of house keys
- Your satellite telephone number, cellular telephone number, web page address and itinerary
- Emergency telephone numbers: parents, plumber, electrician, veterinarian, local police and dog squad, alarm company, electric gate repairs, garden service, lawyer, domestic worker etc.
- Where to find the electricity mains inside and outside the house

- Where to switch off the water mains
- How to operate the alarm
- Knowledge about any guns on the property
- Location of fire extinguishers
- Bin day
- Details on accounts to be paid: rent, electricity, water, rates, alarm, domestic worker, gardener, garden service, telephone, DSTV etc.
- A supply of candles, matches and a torch
- Pet care
- Introduction to neighbours
- Extra money for unforeseen expenses

Do not use both feet to test the depth of the river.

You can't run away from your backside.

African Proberbs

SUPPLIES

Lake Tanganyika

ROUTE PLANNING

1   Our Journey at a Glance

2   Zambia

3   Malawi

4   Tanzania

5   Uganda

6   Kenya

7   Ethiopia

OUR JOURNEY THROUGH EASTERN AFRICA

Total distance travelled: 45 000 kilometres

Total fuel cost: R42 000.00

Total vehicle repairs: R40 000.00

Total number of flat tyres: 30

(The above costs were incurred by one vehicle at the time of our journey.
They have been included here to give you an idea of how expensive this adventure can become)

Currency Converter

		RAND	DOLLAR	POUND
Ethiopia **Birr1.00**		1.49	21.16	32.11
Kenya **KSh1.00**		7.24	102.33	155.27
Malawi **MK1.00**		41.35	593.06	899.90
Tanzania **TSh1.00**		152.17	2174.10	3297.38
Uganda **USh1.00**		237.79	3374.40	5118.85
Zambia **KWa1.00**		891.27	5251.28	19105.72

At time of going to print. Exchange rates are subject to constant fluctuation.

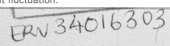

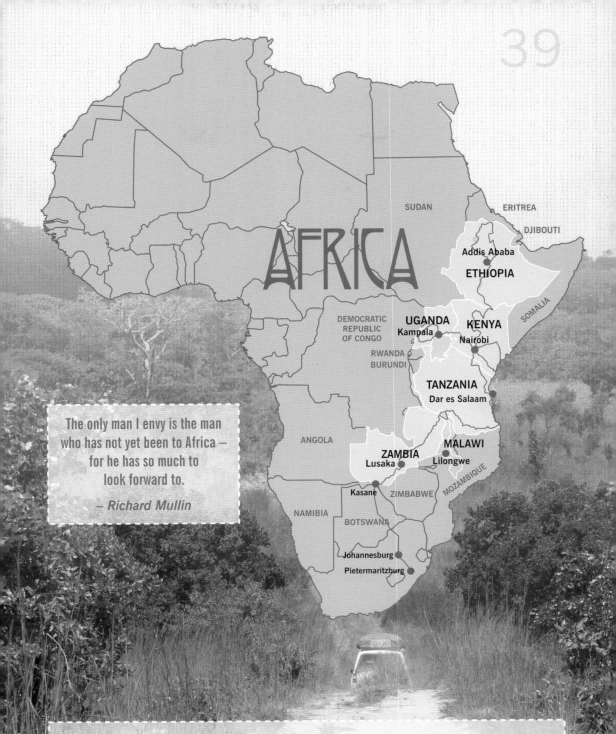

AFRICA

SUDAN

ERITREA

DJIBOUTI

Addis Ababa

ETHIOPIA

DEMOCRATIC
REPUBLIC
OF CONGO

UGANDA

Kampala

KENYA

Nairobi

RWANDA

BURUNDI

SOMALIA

TANZANIA

Dar es Salaam

ANGOLA

MALAWI

ZAMBIA

Lilongwe

Lusaka

MOZAMBIQUE

Kasane

ZIMBABWE

NAMIBIA

BOTSWANA

Johannesburg

Pietermaritzburg

The only man I envy is the man
who has not yet been to Africa —
for he has so much to
look forward to.

– Richard Mullin

I have travelled the length and breadth of this country, met people, spoken to
the children, the aged, everyone I could touch or see. Everyone seeks peace.
Everyone seeks a better life. Everyone wants to work together.

– Nelson Mandela

■ The Forgotten

Animal abuse and neglect is a common sight in eastern Africa, and can be distressing for animal lovers.

No one must shut his eyes and regard as non-existent the suffering of which he spares himself the sight. While so much ill-treatment of animals goes on, we all share the guilt.

– Dr Albert Schweitzer

What is man without the beasts? If all the beasts were gone, man would die from a great loneliness of spirit. For whatever happens to the beasts, happens to man. All things are connected.

– Chief Seattle

ROUTE PLANNING

■ Our Environment

Of all the countries we visited, Kenya showed the most severe signs of soil erosion and land degradation.

However, attempts are being made to educate the public **(right)**.

DESERTIFICATION AND CLIMATE CHANGE ONE GLOBAL CHALLENGE

Combating Desertification and Climate change

CAUSES

- Overgrazing
- Unsustainable agricultural activities
- Deforestation
- Increase in human population
- Insecurity
- Mining and quarrying

ACTIONS

- Sustainable use of natural resources
- Building local capacity
- Awareness creation
- Increase market opportunities
- Resource mobilization through public/ private partnership
- Acquisition and adoption of appropriate livelihood systems
- Value addition to products

■ Memorable Faces of eastern Africa

Ingenious Ways to Use a Bicycle!

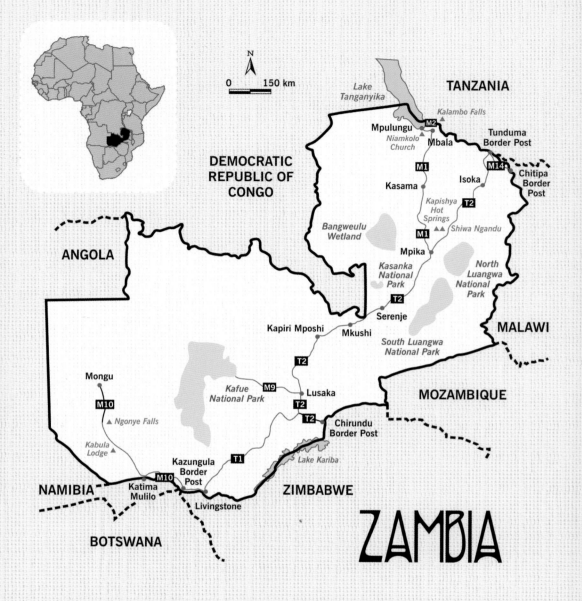

ZAMBIA

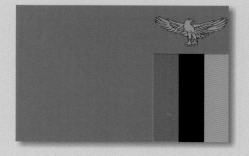

The green represents agriculture, and the orange represents the country's copper resources. Red represents the struggle for freedom while the black represents the African people of Zambia. The African Fish Eagle is from the country's official coat of arms and represents the Zambian people's ability to rise above the nation's problems.

■ Zambia at a Glance

- Highlights included Kabula Lodge, Bangweule Wetland, Shiwa Ngandu, Kapishya Hot Springs, Kalambo Falls and Isanga Bay Lodge on Lake Tanganyika.

- The border posts are confusing and chaotic. Keep a close eye on your valuables at the Tunduma border post.

- Diesel was widely available but expensive.

- The main roads are in good condition but deteriorate the further north you go. On a recent trip through Zambia, the T2 had started to deteriorate as far south as Serenje. Some of the potholes are dangerously deep and wide. We reported one such pothole and were told, 'This is Zambia.' Excellent road signage. Watch out for speeding buses.

- Police roadblocks occur on a regular basis. Have your border forms and international driving license ready for inspection. No bribery was experienced.

- Lusaka was clean with supermarkets, banks and ATM facilities.

- Fruit and vegetables are available for purchase from roadside stalls.

- Thick uninhabited bush still exists in Zambia and makes an ideal campsite if you need to watch your spending.

- The local people are very friendly and we did not experience any crime.

■ General Information

Airlines

South African Airways
Southern Sun, Church Hill Road, Lusaka
Tel: (211) 254350

British Airways
Corporate Park, Alick Nkata Road, Lusaka
Tel: (211) 250579

Automobile Association

Mulungushi Conference Centre,
Great East Road, Lusaka
Tel: (211) 290981
E-mail: info@aazambia.com
Web: www.aazambia.com

Border Crossing

Carbon Tax: KWa200 000.00
Council Levy: KWa25 000.00
Road Tax: US$30.00
Third Party Insurance: KWa150 000.00
(valid for one month only)

Visas are not required for South African
passport holders.
Web: www.zambiaimmigration.gov.zm

Climate

The summer rains fall between November and
April with daytime temperatures averaging
around 32°C. Dirt Roads may become
impassable and mosquitos are more
prevalent. It is very hot in the Zambezi and
Luangwa valleys between December and
October. The winter rains fall between June
and August with daytime temperatures
averaging around 20°C. The sparse vegetation
and lack of water makes this an ideal time to
view game.

Diplomatic Missions

South Africa
26D Cheetah Road, Kabulonga, Lusaka
Tel: (211) 262119
E-mail: zahc@zamnet.zm

United Kingdom
5210 Independence Avenue, Lusaka
Tel: (211) 251133/423200
E-mail: LusakaGeneralEnquiries@fco.gov.uk

Malawi
31 Bishop's Road, Lusaka
Tel: (211) 265768
E-mail: mhcomm@iwayafrica.com

ZAMBIA – ROUTE PLANNING

Kazangula Ferry

Electricity

The electrical supply is the 220/240 volt system and the three-pin-plugs used are of the British square bayonet pin type.

Kazungula Ferry

Web: www.gov.bw
GPS: S17°47.625' E25°15.737'

Twenty eight American dollars (US$28.00) per vehicle one way. Payment to be made in Kwacha if driving a Zambian-registered vehicle.

Two ferries operate seven days a week from 06:00 to 18:00, including public holidays.

Medical

Compulsory vaccinations: Yellow Fever.
Recommended vaccinations: Hepatitis A & B, Meningitis, Rabies, Tetanus and Typhoid.
Precautions: Malaria risk.

Fairview Hospital
Cnr Church and Chilubi Road, Fairview, Lusaka
Tel: (211) 373000

Medical Air Rescue
Tel: (211) 702664/236644

Money

The unit of currency is the Kwacha (KWa). Coins are no longer in use.

ATMs are only available in the larger towns and cities.

Public Holidays

New Year's Day	– January 01
Women's Day	– March 09
Youth Day	– March 12
Easter	– Variable
Labour Day	– May 01
African Freedom Day	– May 25
Heroes' Day	– First Monday in July
Unity Day	– First Tuesday in July
Farmers' Day	– First Monday in August
Independence Day	– October 24
Christmas Day	– December 25
Boxing Day	– December 26

Rules of the Road and Vehicle Requirements

Drive on the left-hand side of the road. Visitors may drive for up to three months on a valid driving license that has been issued in their country of residence.

ROUTE PLANNING – ZAMBIA

Abandoned steam train, southern Zambia

The speed limit is 50 kilometres per hour in built-up areas and 100 kilometres per hour on the open road. This may vary as per the regulatory traffic signs.

Have your border documents on hand for the numerous police roadblocks.

You will need two small red rectangular reflective strips at the back, on the left and right side of the vehicle, with white reflective strips on the front. You will also need a ZA sticker and two emergency triangles, which must be on a metal plate.

A fire extinguisher is compulsory if carrying fuel in jerry cans.

The use of a mobile phone whilst driving is prohibited.

Service Telephone Numbers and Area Codes

International Code for Zambia: +260

Area Codes: Chipata 216, Kasama 214, Livingstone 213, Lusaka 211, Mongu 218, Solwezi 217.

Ambulance and Police Emergency Service – Tel: 999/112
Police – Tel: 991
Operator – Tel: 102/100

Vehicle Assistance

Toyota
Cairo Road, North End, Lusaka
Tel: (211) 229109/228228

Autoworld Ltd
Freedom Way, Lusaka
Tel: (211) 260211/237716

Land Rover – Alliance Motors
Plot 9219, Ben Bella Road, Lusaka
Tel: (211) 847991/846917

Websites and Books for Additional Information

Web: www.africa-in-sights.com/zambia
www.travelafrica.com
www.zambiatourism.com
www.shiwangandu.com

'Beat about the Bush – Mammals' by Trevor Carnaby
'Beat about the Bush – Birds' by Trevor Carnaby
'The Africa House: The Story of an English Gentleman and his African Dream' by Christina Lamb

ZAMBIA – ROUTE PLANNING

- Many tsetse flies 'hitch a ride' on the back of the vehicle and make a dash for the windows when the vehicle stops. We covered the back of the vehicle with a household spray for flying and crawling insects. This helped to a certain extent. Use window screens, stand still if out in the open, apply lots of insect repellant and wear light shaded clothing in green, cream and brown. Good luck!

■ Kazungula Border Post to Kabula Lodge

It is approximately 203 kilometres from the Kazungula border post to Kabula Lodge.

Fuel is expensive in Zambia so it would be advisable to fill up prior to entry.

From the border post proceed to the main road. Take a left onto the M10 (a good tar road) to Katima. From here, continue north along the M10 to Mongu for roughly 58 kilometres. This is now a tarred road in good condition.

We had originally planned to go to Mongu and then on to the Kafue National Park. However, the Zambezi River was in flood at the time and the ferry crossing to Mongu had been closed. The group decided to stay at Kabula Lodge for several days to unwind before proceeding.

Kabula Lodge

South Africa – Tel: +27 (0) 826725168
E-mail: info@kabulalodge.com
(attention Piet du Toit)
Web: www.kabulalodge.com
GPS: S17°03.281' E024°00.125'

Situated on the banks of the mighty Zambezi River with beautiful grassed campsites under huge indigenous trees, clean ablutions, hot water and good security. Tiger fishing, bird watching, walks in the surrounding indigenous forest, canoeing and rafting available. Fishing boats for hire. Camping costs R115.00 per person per day.

Kabula Lodge campsite

ROUTE PLANNING – ZAMBIA

COLOURFUL TRADE NAMES

- Hop In Bar
- Supernatural Boutique
- Gift of God Investment

- Free Paying Toilet
- Anaconda Fishing Worms
- Black Out Night Club

Lost en route to Kafue National Park

Ngonye Falls

If it wasn't for Victoria Falls, the Ngonye Falls would be a major attraction. Approximately 74 kilometres from Kabula Lodge, heading north on the M10, to Mongu.

The turnoff is clearly marked and there is ample space to park. A beautiful horseshoe shaped waterfall that cascades over a 20 metre drop. The rocks are sharp so take a good pair of walking shoes, your swimming costume and lunch.

■ Kabula Lodge to Kafue National Park

Web: www.zambiatourism.com

A couple of members in the group decided it would be a good idea to enter Kafue National Park from the south as opposed to going the long way round via Livingstone and Lusaka. This proved to be a bad idea! After three days of driving around in the tsetse fly infested bush, it was agreed that we were definitely lost and would have to retrace our steps back to the main road and follow the route via Livingstone and Lusaka.

ZAMBIA – ROUTE PLANNING

Impassable rivers, thick elephant grass, miomba woodland and, for the first time, tsetse flies. They caught us all by surprise. A few painful bites later we realised we were under attack and war was declared! You cannot just swat these flies; they have to be caught and squashed to a pulp, even when they are half dead they keep coming at you!

Ingrid Hardman

ANGELS IN DISGUISE

As luck would have it, two local men walking along the road, agreed to show us the way – for a bus fare back home!

120 kilometres and eight hours later, we arrived in southern Kafue. It's amazing to see how many people in Africa will go out of their way to help lost travellers. Thank you Alex and Pritchard.

Entry into the Kafue National Park is US$15.00 per vehicle per day and US$20.00 per person per day. Having travelled through the southern section and seen no animals, despite plenty of evidence to their presence, the group decided they had had enough. After a couple of days relaxing at the New Kalala Camp, we moved on to Lusaka.

New Kalala Camp

Tel: (211) 290914
Web: www.newkalala.com

Situated on the banks of the Itezhi-Tezhi Dam, bordering the southern section of the

Kafue National Park. If travelling from Lusaka, take the M9 to Mongu. After 216 kilometres, turn left onto the D769 (Musungwa Road), at GPS reading S14°58.16' E26°27.04'. Follow the dirt road for almost 119 kilometres, to the New Kalala Camp (which is near the Musa entrance gate). What a lovely site.

Camping costs US$15.00 per person per day.

■ Kafue National Park to Lusaka

It is approximately 350 kilometres from the New Kalala Camp to Lusaka.

Retrace your steps back to Lusaka where the M9 will eventually connect with Cairo Road in Lusaka. Take a right onto Cairo Road and proceed for roughly 10 kilometres to the Eureka Camp, clearly marked on the left. Diesel in Lusaka costs KWa7.59 per litre.

There is a shopping mall, Manda Hill Centre, on the corner of Manchichi Road and the Great East Road. It has a Shoprite Checkers, Game, Celtel, pharmacy, hardware and photographic shop.

SCHOOL MOTTOES

- Education for Self Reliance
- Strive to Achieve
- Education for a Better Tomorrow
- Success through Hard Work

Eureka Camp

Tel: (211) 278110
E-mail: eurekacamp.zm@gmail.com
Web: www.eurekacamp.com

Situated on the Kafue Road, 10 kilometres south of the southern traffic circle at GPS reading S15°30.261' E28°15.583'. Not much grass, with a fair amount of shade. Clean ablutions with hot water. Close to all amenities. Good spot for vehicle repairs, laundry and re-stocking. Camping costs US$7.00 per person per day. This camp is often frequented by backpackers who can be very inconsiderate, so choose your campsite carefully.

■ Lusaka to Forest Inn

It is approximately 273 kilometres from Lusaka to Forest Inn.

Proceed through Lusaka, on the Great North Road (T2), for 200 kilometres to Kapiri Mposhi. This section of the road is very good except for the odd pothole easily recognisable by the skid marks that precede them! Continue along the T2 for a further 63 kilometres to Forest Inn.

MANDA HILL CENTRE – LUSAKA

Cream Crackers 200g – KWa8 990.00
Bokomo Cornflakes 500g – KWa16 990.00
Smooth Yoghurt 500ml – KWa9 990.00
Tomato & Onion Mix   – KWa10 990.00
410g

Most shops in Zambia carry the same range of familiar groceries found in South Africa.

... talking a lot of bullshit, and spitting out words from the dictionary he'd swallowed. It turned out he was just a facilitator who knew bugger all! Eissshhh, I was fuming!

Ingrid, trying to sort out her Comesa Yellow Card in the wrong building!

Diesel costs KWa7.60 per litre in Kapiri Mposhi.

Tomatoes, cabbage, sweet potatoes, bananas, lemons, pumpkins, beans, ground nuts, watermelon and charcoal are for sale en route.

Forest Inn

Tel: (215) 353000
E-mail: forestinn@iwayafrica.com
Web: www.forestinn-zambia.com

30 kilometres south of Mkushi town and 63 kilometres north of the Kapiri Mposhi T-junction. Clearly marked on the right. Beautiful grassed campsites under shady indigenous trees. Clean ablutions with hot water. Small restaurant and bar. Trails into the pristine miombo woodland with the possibility of seeing the chestnut-mantled sparrow-weaver and the boehm's flycatcher. Beautiful spot. Well worth the stay. Camping costs KWa60.00 per person per day.

■ Forest Inn to Kasanka National Park

It is approximately 236 kilometres from Forest Inn to Kasanka National Park.

Continue north along the T2 for 181 kilometres to the D235. Turn left onto the D235, a good dirt road, and proceed for a further 55 kilometres to the Kasanka National Park entrance gate, marked on the left.

En route you may like to stop and view the Kundilila Falls north of Serenje.

Diesel was available in Serenje.

Kasanka National Park

E-mail: trust@kasanka.com
Web: www.kasanka.com

Kasanka is a privately managed national park that has an abundance of game, of which the reddish-brown sitatunga is the star attraction. Between November and December, be sure to see the biggest gathering of migratory, giant fruit bats in the world. Our campsite, Fibwe Hide, was nestled in-between a copse of beautiful trees with ample shade. Our private camp assistant brought daily supplies of water and lit the camp fire every night. Rustic shower with cold water. Well worth the stay. The entrance fee is US$10.00 per person per day and US$15.00 per vehicle per day. Camping costs US$15.00 per person per day.

Not only does each zebra have its own stripe pattern, but the left and right sides are different too. This unique pattern enables the foal and its mother to identify each other in the first few days after birth. It is not clear which part of the pattern is memorised. Some say it may be the face pattern or the shoulder pattern.

Kundilila Falls

Approximately 61 kilometres north of Serenje on the T2. GPS reading S13°04.207' E30°48.050'. There is a signpost, but it is in a bad state of disrepair, so keep your eyes open! Turn right onto a good dirt road and travel for 13 kilometres to the parking lot. A guide will accompany you to the bottom of the falls (65 metres down), but be warned: the walk back up is not for the physically unfit! There is a beautiful pool at the bottom, so don't forget your swimming costume. Camping is permitted but there are no facilities.

■ Kasanka National Park to Bangweulu Wetland

It is approximately 339 kilometres from Kasanka National Park to Bangweulu Wetland.

This is an amazing place and should be one of your top destinations to visit. Retrace your steps back to the T2 and head north towards Mpika. At GPS reading S12°16.936' E31°08.026', turn left onto a rough dirt road, which could become problematic in the rainy season.

En route to Bangweulu Wetland

Proceed for approximately 120 kilometres at 15 to 20 kilometres per hour. You will need to pass through three gate posts and take a right at the one and only fork in the road. Due to the high population density en route, it would be advisable to get an early start since possible campsites are few and far between.

As you begin to approach the base camp, the bush will fall away to reveal a magnificent plain stretching as far as the eye can see. The road proceeds onto a 3 metre wide causeway, but this is for pedestrians only. You will be required to proceed into the muddy water and follow the causeway to the base camp (right). Despite the copious amount of mud and water the ground underneath is fairly hard.

I walked along the high track to watch the sunrise, and my mood from the day before lifted when I saw the breathtaking vista before me ... orange clouds scudded to the east with the moon still visible in the west, and for 360 degrees one could see thousands of black lechwe, flocks of wattled crane, ibis and cormorants. It was absolute magic!

One of my best moments so far.

Ingrid Hardman

Should your vehicle start to slow down, despite the pedal to the metal, do not panic! There is nothing mechanically wrong – it is only a ton of weed attaching itself to the undercarriage! Once you reach the base camp, remove the weed, don your Wellingtons, gather your clothes and food and proceed across the shallow swamp to the makoro and, finally, Shoebill Island.

The following morning, the local guide will take you on a makoro ride through the wetland in search of the famous shoebill stork. The best time of the year to visit is between May and July, as the water starts to recede thereafter.

The entrance fee is US$10.00 per person per day and US$15.00 per vehicle per day.

Accommodation is in the form of tents and rustic chalets for US$83.00 per person per day. Camping is only possible during the dry season (July – October) and costs US$22.00 per person per night.

E-mail: trust@kasanka.com
Web: www.kasanka.com.

Arriving at Shoebill Island

ROUTE PLANNING – ZAMBIA

■ Bangweulu Wetland to Shiwa Ngandu

It is approximately 450 kilometres from the Bangweulu Wetland to Shiwa Ngandu.

Make your way back to the T2 and take a left turn to Mpika 150 kilometres away. Continue along the T2 for a further 90 kilometres until you see the sign for Shiwa Ngandu (S11°13.329ⁱ E31°49.575ⁱ). Follow the dirt road to Shiwa Ngandu and the campsite at Kapishya Hot Springs.

Diesel was available in Mpika for KWa2 100.00 per litre. There was also an Auto Trader and Commercial Bank.

Shiwa Ngandu

Web: www.shiwangandu.com

Shiwa Ngandu is a stately manor house set in formal gardens – a slice of England in the middle of Africa. Overlooking the Lake of the Royal Crocodile, Shiwa Ngandu was completed by Sir Stewart Gore-Brown in 1932, and is now run by his grandson. This is an amazing place and definitely worth the visit. Guided tours are given between 09:00 and 11:00 at a cost of US$20.00 per person.

Shiwa Ngandu

Kapishya Hot Springs

Cell: 0976970444
E-mail: kapishya@shiwasafaris.com
(attention Mark)
Web: www.shiwasafaris.com

Lovely campsite with lots of shade and green grass; situated on the banks of the Mansha River. Clean ablutions with ample hot water. The hot springs, at no extra charge, are in close proximity to the camp. Bar and restaurant up at the lodge. Camping costs US$15.00 per person per day.

Sir Stewart Gore-Brown

■ Shiwa Ngandu to Mpulungu

It is approximately 376 kilometers from Kapishya Hot Springs to Mpulungu.

We followed the dirt road west from Kapishya Hot Springs, for 45 kilometres, to meet up with the M1 north to Kasama.

As you enter Kasama, take a right turn at the stop street and proceed to Mbala/Mpulungu.

Diesel was available in Kasama with a Shoprite and ATM that would only take a Visa Card.

From here on, the M1 becomes badly potholed and it will take approximately four hours to cover 175 kilometres at less than 40 kilometres an hour! At the T-junction, take a left to Mpulungu, and continue for a further 33 kilometres. Take a right turn, after 'Hopes Kitchen,' and proceed along a dirt road past the fisheries to Nkupi Lodge.

ROUTE PLANNING – ZAMBIA

Fine English crockery carefully transported over rough seas and through thick bush to grace the table at Shiwa Ngandu

Nkupi Lodge

Tel: (214) 455166

The campsite is surrounded by a beautiful garden with lots of green grass, ample shade and clean ablutions with cold water. Camping costs US$15.00 per person per day.

Niamkolo Church

From the lodge, continue up the hill for a short distance to Zambia's oldest surviving church. It was built in 1895 by the London Missionary Society and although the roof has long gone, the walls still remain. Entry is free.

■ Mpulungu to Lake Tanganyika

It is approximately 90 kilometres from Mpulungu to Isanga Bay Lodge.

Retrace your steps back to the T-junction and proceed on to Mbala. Once in Mbala, pass through the traffic circle and continue for 6.4 kilometres, where you will need to take a left turn. Continue for 17 kilometres. At this point, you can either continue on to Kalambo Falls (approximately 13 kilometres away), or take a left turn to Isanga Bay Lodge. Although the distance to Isanga Bay Lodge is only 20 kilometres it took us three hours to cover! On our arrival, we were met with looks of astonishment, as the road had been closed for almost six months! Fortunately for you, the road is now open!

Diesel costs KWa8.59 per litre in Mbala.

Isanga Bay Lodge

Cell: 0966646991
E-mail: bookings@isangabay.com
Web: www.isangabaylodge.com

This is a lovely spot to spend several days relaxing. The campsite has plenty of shade, clean ablutions and an amazing view over Lake Tanganyika.

Camping costs US$20.00 per person per day.

Kalambo Falls

Kalambo Falls is over twice the height of Victoria Falls. It is the second highest single drop (221 metres) waterfall in Africa and the 12th highest in the world! There is a narrow walkway from which you can view the falls from several different angles. Well worth the visit. Camping is permitted but there are no facilities.

EXCERPT FROM A LETTER SENT HOME

We stopped off to see Zambia's oldest church and then headed for Isanga Bay Lodge, blissfully unaware that the road had been closed for a long time with access now by boat. The track was 20 kilometres of pure hell … steep, narrow, littered with boulders and fallen trees that needed to be cut and winched aside in the blistering heat of the day. We so desperately wanted to believe there was an alternate route we had somehow missed. But as luck would have it, there wasn't one and we would have to pass this way again on our way out! This was just a taste of what was to come!

Lake Tanganyika to the Tunduma Border Post and Malawi

It is approximately 284 kilometres from Mbala to Malawi.

We stopped to view Kalambo Falls on our return from Isanga Bay Lodge. From there we headed into Mbala, and due to the late hour, decided to spend the night at the 'Grasshopper Inn.' We took a room (much to everyone's horror) to get out of the pouring rain, and although it was pretty much in a state of disrepair, we had a good night's sleep with no bug bites or other ailments to show for it!

The following morning we proceeded back down the M1 and after a short distance took a left turn onto the D1. After 176 kilometres, this good dirt road connects you with the T2. From there we proceeded to the Tunduma border post to exit Zambia. Once that was done, we took the M14, a good dirt road, to Malawi. Diesel costs KWa17.70 per litre in Tunduma.

Kalambo Falls

Sunset over Lake Tanganyika

ROUTE PLANNING – ZAMBIA

Most local shops in Zambia stock a wide variety of groceries!

Chitipa Border Post

M26

Songwe Border Post
Karonga

M1

Chilumba
Livingstonia

TANZANIA

Nyika
National
Park

Mzuzu

ZAMBIA

Lake Malawi

MOZAMBIQUE

0   100 km

Lilongwe

MOZAMBIQUE

Blantyre

MALAWI

MALAWI – ROUTE PLANNING

The black stripe on the national flag of Malawi represents the African people; the red represents the blood of martyrs for African freedom; the green represents Malawi's evergreen nature and the rising sun represents the dawn of freedom and hope for Africa.

■ Malawi at a Glance

- Fuel is only available in the main towns and cities.
- There is ample accommodation along the shores of Lake Malawi.
- Roads and road signs are in good condition.
- Fruit and vegetables are available for purchase from roadside stalls.
- The local people are very friendly.
- Although the local shops stock a wide variety of goods, only the larger towns and cities offer supermarket facilities and ATM access.

Yeah right!

■ General Information

Airlines

South African Airways
Lilongwe – Tel: (01) 772242

British Airways
Lilongwe – Tel: (01) 771747/754950

Air Malawi
Lilongwe – Tel: (01) 700811

Automobile Association

Next to Old Town Mall, Lilongwe
Tel: (01) 750245
Breakdown: 0999447447
E-mail: admin@aamalawi.com
Web: www.aamalawi.com

The forest looks thick;
when you come closer
you can see that every
tree is standing on its own.

African Proverb

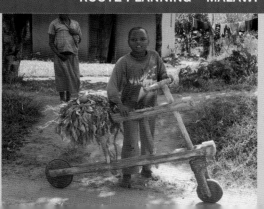

Border Crossing

Temporary Import Permit: R150.00
Third Party Insurance: R700.00

All borders close at 18:00 except Mchinji border post, which is open 24 hours a day. No visa is required for South African passport holders.
Web: www.immigration.gov.mw
Web: www.malawiembassy.org

Citi Info

A free monthly guide on what is happening in Malawi with comprehensive maps, useful telephone numbers, accommodation details and tourist information. Copies can be found in supermarkets and shops.

Climate

The summer rains fall between November and April with daytime temperatures averaging around 32°C. Dirt Roads may become impassable and mosquitos are more prevalent. The dry winter season falls between June and October with daytime temperatures averaging around 25°C. Night-time temperatures in the Nyika National Park can be as low as 2°C.

Diplomatic Missions

South Africa
3rd floor, Kangombe House,
Robert Mugabe Crescent, Lilongwe
Tel: (01) 773722
E-mail: sahc@malawi.net

United Kingdom
Lilongwe – Tel: (01) 772400
E-mail: bhclilongwe@fco.gov.uk

Tanzania
Plaza House, Lilongwe
Tel: (01) 775035,
E-mail: tzhc@malawi.net

Electricity

The electricity supply is 220–230 volts single phase or 380–400 volts three phase. Plugs for appliances are the square-three-pin British pattern.

Medical

Compulsory vaccinations: None.
Recommended vaccinations: Hepatitis A & B, Polio, Rabies, Tetanus and Typhoid.
Precautions: Malaria risk.

Discovery Medi-Clinic
Lilongwe – Tel: (01) 776082

MALAWI – ROUTE PLANNING

DID YOU KNOW?

According to African legend, the baobab wanted to become the most beautiful tree of all. When it realised this was not possible, it put its head into the ground so that only the roots pointed heavenwards. Another legend tells us that when the baobab was planted by God, it kept walking. God then pulled it up and replanted it upside down to stop it from moving!

Money

The unit of currency is the Malawian Kwacha (MK).

Public Holidays

New Year's Day – January 01
Chilembwe Day – January 15
Martyrs' Day – March 03
Easter – Variable
Labour Day – May 01
Freedom Day – June 14
Independance Day – July 06
Christmas Day – December 25
Boxing Day – December 26

Rules of the Road and Vehicle Requirements

Drive on the left-hand side of the road.

Visitors may drive for up to three months on a valid driving license that has been issued in their country of residence.

All vehicles must carry two warning triangles and a ZA sticker.

The speed limit is 50 kilometres per hour in built up areas and 80 kilometres per hour on the open road. This may vary as per the regulatory traffic signs.

Service Telephone Numbers and Area Codes

International Code for Malawi: +265

Ambulance – Tel: 998
Police Rapid Response – Tel: 997
Operator – Tel: 100
International Operator – Tel: 102
Directory Enquiries – Tel: 191

Vehicle Assistance

Toyota Malawi
Off Murray Road, Lilongwe
Tel: (01) 755666

Land Rover
M.A. & Sons, Shire Building,
Chilambula Road, Lilongwe
Tel: (01) 755301

Websites and Books for Additional Information

Web: www.goafrica.about.com
www.malawitourism.com

'Malawi Cichlids in their Natural Habitat' by A. D. Konings

The baobab grows to a height of 22 metres and the circumference of the trunk can measure up to 10 metres. The dry pulp of the long cucumber-shaped fruit is edible and its seeds produce oil. The tree sheds its leaves in the dry season to reduce evaporation.

■ Chitipa Border Post to Sangilo Lodge

It is approximately 177 kilometres from the Chitipa border post to Sangilo Lodge in Chilumba.

The initial plan had been to cross over into Malawi from eastern Zambia via the Chipata/Mchinji border posts. Unexpected floods at the time resulted in the closure of the Luangwa National Park, and as most of us had already been to Lake Malawi, the group decided to enter Malawi from the north via the Chitipa border post.

From the border post we continued along the M26, a fairly good dirt road, to Karonga approximately 87 kilometres away.

Fuel was available in Karonga, as well as ATM and Internet facilities.

We then continued south along the M1, a good tar road, to Chilumba approximately 90 kilometres away.

DID YOU KNOW?

The museum at Karonga is the home of Malawisaurus, a huge dinosaur whose skeleton was found nearby. Karonga is also the site of a World War I battle between the British and the Germans.

Sangilo Lodge

Cell: 0999395203
Web: www.sangilo.net

It's hard not to stay a few days longer when you have campsites situated under shady trees, clean ablutions with hot water and a private beach with its own pub and mini-restaurant. Sangilo Lodge is a hidden gem well worth the visit.

Camping costs US$6.00 per person per day.

MALAWI – ROUTE PLANNING

We saw a couple of strange sights today.

There is a lot of road construction going on. The piles of rock that need to be crushed into smaller stones is all done by hand! Men sit on the roadside with piles of rocks that they hammer into smaller stones – all day!

Bunches of fish are tied onto windshield wipers to dry in the sun. Rice is grown in the marshes on the side of the road and there are lots of huge green chameleons!

Ingrid Hardman

Nyika National Park – beautiful scenery, wild animals and an interesting array of mosses and wild flowers.

Attractions

Livingstonia

A Victorian village in the middle of Africa. It was built on a plateau that overlooks Lake Malawi – in an attempt to avoid malaria, prevalent along the lakeshore below. It is the site of one of the earliest Christian missions and is of great historical interest. The road from the lakeshore via Chitimba affords spectacular views over the lake to the Livingstone Mountains in Tanzania.

Nyika National Park

Tel: (01) 771393
E-mail: reservations@cawsmw.com
Web: www.cawsmw.com

From Chilumba, it will take a full day of driving to get to the campsite, which is very basic with cold water showers. At 2 400 metres the evenings here are bitterly cold.

Camping costs US$15.00 per person per day, US$10.00 per person per day entry and US$3.00 per vehicle per day.

We went for a game drive and saw roan antelope, zebra, bushbuck, warthog and a variety of birds. I also heard a nightjar I have never heard before. We drove back to camp as the sun set, the landscape was softly transformed to pale blues, greens and pinks. Everyone dressed warmly and for the first time on the trip I wore a fleece jacket and my sheepskin slippers that I had packed as an afterthought! Temperatures were dropping fast and the wind-chill made it even colder.

Ingrid Hardman

Lake Malawi

■ Nyika National Park to the Songwe Border Post andTanzania

Make your way back to Chilumba and head north on the M1 to Karonga and the Songwe border post. Once cleared, follow the M1 north to Tanzania, approximately 51 kilometres away.

DID YOU KNOW?

Lake Malawi contains the largest number of fish species of any lake in the world.

We pulled in at a sign for a waterfall view site and our guide informed us that these were a) the highest in Malawi b) not a very steep walk and c) only 20 minutes away … BOLLOCKS! We got back to the car park three bloody hours later!

The first 15 minutes were OK, thereafter it became increasingly slippery and difficult. Very quickly the hike turned into a contest to see who would be the only person not to land on his or her butt!

Only Neville persevered and was rewarded with the view of a piffling 10 metre waterfall!

We got back to the vehicles and made a beeline for a camp on the lakeshore, parked and went straight into the sea … clobber an' all!

Ingrid Hardman

Traditional basket bridge over the South Rukuru River, Kandewe Village

COLOURFUL TRADE NAMES

- Energy Coffins
- Hopeful Discount Retail Shop
- You Never Know General Dealers
- Stone Tyres
- Help Me God Cooking Oil
- Thirsty Pub
- Black Out Night Club

ROUTE PLANNING – MALAWI

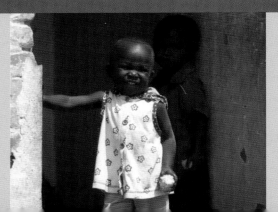

We headed north again to Karonga to stock up on diesel, water and groceries before heading for the Tanzanian border post – a big surprise ... it was organised and efficient and quick by African standards, only took us two hours to pass! Tanzania had completely different topography to Malawi. It is mountainous and lush with massive banana and tea plantations intermingled on the slopes.

Ingrid Hardman

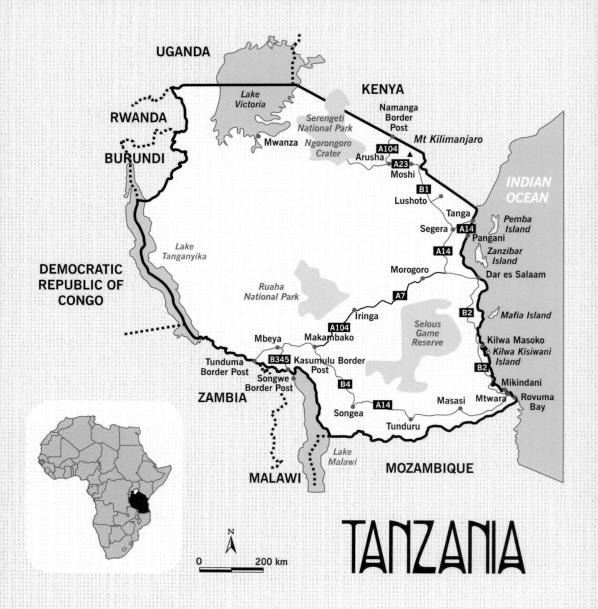

UGANDA

KENYA

Lake Victoria

Serengeti National Park

Namanga Border Post

Mt Kilimanjaro

RWANDA

Mwanza

Ngorongoro Crater

A104 Arusha

A23 Moshi

INDIAN OCEAN

BURUNDI

B1 Lushoto

Tanga

Pemba Island

Segera **A14**
Pangani

A14

Zanzibar Island

DEMOCRATIC REPUBLIC OF CONGO

Lake Tanganyika

Morogoro

Dar es Salaam

Ruaha National Park

A7

Iringa

Selous Game Reserve

B2

Mafia Island

A104 Makambako

Mbeya

Kilwa Masoko
Kilwa Kisiwani Island

Tunduma Border Post

B345 Kasumulu Border Post

B2

Mikindani

Songwe Border Post

B4

Masasi

Mtwara

Rovuma Bay

ZAMBIA

Songea

A14

Tunduru

Lake Malawi

MOZAMBIQUE

MALAWI

N

0   200 km

TANZANIA

The Tanzanian national flag is derived from the flags of Tanganyika and Zanzibar. The green represents the natural vegetation, the yellow represents rich mineral deposits; the black represents the native Swahili people of Tanzania while the blue represents the numerous lakes, rivers and the Indian Ocean.

■ Tanzania at a Glance

- Highlights included Kilwa Kisiwani, Zanzibar, Pangani, Lushoto, Serengeti National Park and the Ngorongoro Crater.

- Crime prevails in Arusha.

- Roads and signage generally good.

- Good value for money accommodation on Zanzibar Island. Negotiable in the low season.

- Good snorkelling at the village of Ruvula on the Msimbati peninsula near Mtwara.

- The B2 is now tarred and there is a bridge over the Rufiji River.

- Trucks and buses are a danger on the road.

- The A14, a dirt track between Songea and Mtwara, should be avoided in the rainy season.

- The Tunduma border post between Zambia and Tanzania is a nightmare! Keep valuables out of sight and appoint at least two members of the group to watch the vehicles.

- As a group of four vehicles and eight adults, it worked out cheaper to leave our vehicles at the Meserani Snake Park and take a three day, two night all-inclusive package tour into the Ngorongoro Crater and Serengeti National Park.

- Early morning and late evening can be cold in the winter season.

- Coartem tablets, for the treatment of malaria, are available at a good price throughout Tanzania.

- There are still plenty of wild open spaces to 'bushcamp'.

- In order to park in Tanzanian towns and cities, you will need to purchase a parking ticket from one of the many ticket sellers roaming the streets. This ticket entitles you to a day's parking in that particular town, and once purchased, it should be displayed on the windscreen.

- Most accommodation along the coast is closed mid-year due to the trade winds and copious amount of seaweed washed ashore.

Below: German boma window, Mikindani

ROUTE PLANNING – TANZANIA

■ General Information

Airlines

South African Airways
Tel: (022) 2117045

Air Tanzania
Tel: (022) 2117500

Kenya Airways
Tel: (022) 2119376

**Julius Nyerere international Airport
Information Desk**
Tel: (022) 2844211/2

Automobile Association

Morogoro Road, Dar es Salaam
Tel: (022) 2151837
E-mail: info@aatanzania.org

Border Crossing

Road Tax per vehicle: US$25.00
(valid for one month)
Third Party Insurance: TSh150 000.00

The 'road' between Songea and Mtwara in southern Tanzania!

A visa is required for South African passport holders. A single entry visa, valid for three months from the date of entry, will cost US$50.00 per person.
Web: www.tanzaniaconsul.com

Climate

The summer rains fall between March and May with daytime temperatures averaging 32°C. Dirt Roads may become impassable and mosquitos are more prevalent. The short rains fall between November and December. The dry season, between June and October, is the best time to visit with daytime temperatures averaging 20°C. The sparse vegetation and lack of water makes this an ideal time to view game.

Diplomatic Missions

South Africa

Plot 1338, Mwaya Road, Dar es Salaam
Tel: (022) 2601800
E-mail: sahc.tanzania@dirco.gov.za

United Kingdom

Umoja House, Hamburg Avenue, Dar es Salaam
Tel: (022) 2110102
E-mail: bhc.dar@fco.gov.uk

Uganda

25 Msasani Road, Oysterbay, Dar es Salaam
Tel: (022) 2667391
E-mail: info@ughc.co.tz

Electricity

Tanzania uses the 220–240 volt system. Plugs and sockets vary but are mostly the British three-square-pin or two-round-pin variety.

Ferry to Zanzibar

Departure time from Dar es Salaam to Zanzibar – 07:00, 09:30, 12:30, and 15:45 Departure time from Zanzibar to Dar es Salaam – 07:00, 09:30, 12:30, and 15:30.

When booking, confirm the above departure times, as they are likely to change without notice, especially on Sundays.

US$35.00 per person
US$25.00 per child under 12
25 kilograms per person permitted luggage

The booking office and departure point can be found opposite the Cathedral of St. Joseph, Sokoine Drive, Dar es Salaam.

Azam Marine Co Ltd
Specialists in fast ferry services
Tel: (022) 2123324/2133024
Web: www.azam-marine.com

Medical

Compulsory vaccinations: Yellow Fever.
Recommended vaccinations: Hepatitis A & B,
Meningitis, Tetanus and Typhoid.
Precautions: Malaria risk.

Aga Khan Hospital
Ocean Road, Dar es Salaam
Tel: (022) 2115151/3

Trauma Centre
589 Yacht Club Road, Masasani Peninisula,
Dar es Salaam
Tel: (022) 2602500

Lutheran Medical Hospital – Arusha
Tel: (027) 2548030

Money

The unit of currency is the Tanzanian Shilling
(TSh).

ATMs are available in larger towns and cities.

Public Holidays

New Year's Day	– January 01
Zanzibar Revolution Day	– January 12
Easter	– Variable
Union Day	– April 26
Labour Day	– May 01
Peasants' Day	– July 07
Farmers' Day	– August 08
Nyerere Day	– October 14
Independence Day	– December 09
Christmas Day	– December 25
Boxing Day	– December 26

Rules of the Road and Vehicle Requirements

Drive on the left-hand side of the road.

Visitors may drive for up to three months on
a valid driving license that has been issued in
their country of residence.

The wearing of seatbelts is mandatory.

The speed limit is 50 kilometres per hour in
built-up areas and 100 kilometres per hour
on the open road. This may vary as per the
regulatory traffic signs.

ZA sticker is required.

Service Telephone Numbers and Area Codes

International code for Tanzania: +255

Area codes: Arusha 027, Dar es Salaam 022,
Iringa 026, Mbeya 025, Mtwara 023,
Ruvuma 025, Tanga 027 and Zanzibar 024.

TANZANIA – ROUTE PLANNING

To be without a friend is to
be poor indeed.
Tanzanian Proverb

Ambulance and Police Emergency Service –
Tel: 112/999
Directory Enquiries – Tel: 118

The Slipway

Cell: 0784324044
E-mail: slipway@slipway.net
Web: www.slipway.net.

The Slipway is situated on the Msasani
Peninsula, north of Msimbazi Bay, away
from the busy streets of Dar es Salaam. The
centre offers a restaurant, bookshop, curio
stalls, cellular phone outlet, accommodation
and a ferry service to the Bongoyo Island
Marine Reserve, Zanzibar, Pemba and Mafia
Islands. Fishing trips can also be arranged.

Vehicle Assistance

CMC Land Rover

For genuine Land Rover parts
Maktaba Road, Dar es Salaam
Tel: (022) 2113017

24-hour Roadside Assistance
Cell: 0785828100

Toyota Tanzania

5 Nyerere Road, Dar es Salaam
Tel: (022) 2866815

COLOURFUL TRADE NAMES

- Sweet Bite
- The Old New
- Bite Bar
- Be Used Spares
- Ozone Lodge and Bar
- Mobile Shop
- Up To Date Lodge

Bicycle taxis

Websites and Books for Additional Information

Web: www.tanzaniatouristboard.com
www.tanzaniaparks.com
www.tanzaniatourismonline.com
www.zanzibartourism.net
www.mydestination.com

'Signs of the Wild' by Clive Walker

What's Happening in Dar es Salaam

A free monthly guide on Dar es Salaam, usually found in supermarkets and shops.

Good street map of the city and a wide selection of telephone numbers and ferry departure times.

Visit www.tanzaniatourismonline.com for editions of the Tanzania Travel and Tourism Directory and the Tanzanian Accommodation Guide.

■ Kasumulu Border Post to Mbeya

Despite arriving late in Tanzania, we were fortunate enough to find accommodation at the Karibuni Centre (a school, run by nuns). This school is signposted on the left, about 41 kilometres from the border post.

Otherwise try the Utengule Coffee Lodge
Cell: 0753020901
E-mail: reservations@utengule.com
Web: www.riftvalley-zanzibar.com
GPS: E33°19.24' S8°53.06'

Camping costs US$11.50 per person per day.

Mikindani Bay

Follow the A104 west to Mbeya and Mbalizi. Turn right at the signpost and follow the road for 8.5 kilometres, keeping left at the first fork. The lodge is signposted on the right thereafter.

Mbeya is a very busy town and one in which you can easily get lost! There are banking facilities with ATMs, an Internet café and a couple of shops selling vehicle spares.

Diesel was available in Mbeya at TSh2 200.00 per litre. Avocados, bananas, pineapples and cabbages were also available.

■ Mbeya to the Coastal Town of Mikindani

It is approximately 1 103 kilometres from Mbeya to Mikindani.

This section of road is not for the faint-hearted! Its bad condition tells a story of the hardship and frustration of past travellers caught in the rainy season. It took us three days of hard driving, at an average speed of 21 kilometers per hour, to reach Mikindani. One particular pothole was level with the window of the Land Rover. Be warned!

From Mbeya we took the A104, on good tar, for 149 kilometres to Makambako. About 14 kilometres out of Makambako (just after the BP station), take a right-hand turn to Njombe. Proceed for 307 kilometres on a good tar road with the odd pothole – the number of which will increase as you get closer to Songea!

Diesel was available in Songea.

Pineapples, avocados, potatoes, tomatoes, cabbage and bananas were for sale en route. Watch out for speeding buses.

The tar road ends after Songea and there is no fuel available until Masasi.

Proceed for 300 kilometres to Tunduru and then a further 200 kilometres to Masasi where the tar road begins again. From Masasi we headed to Lindi, 123 kilometres away, and then a further 10 kilometres on to Mikindani.

Camping in the bush along this route is the only available 'accommodation' from Mbeya to Mikindani.

THE REPUTED DWELLING PLACE
OF
Dr DAVID LIVINGSTONE
FROM
24TH MARCH TO 7TH APRIL
1866
FROM HERE HE BEGAN HIS LAST JOURNEY

David Livingstone spent a few weeks in Mikindani in 1866 before setting out on his last journey.

Sunset from Ten Degrees South

Mikindani

Web: www.mikindani.com

Mikindani is a good base from which to explore the surrounding area. Although most books will tell you Mikindani is mostly of historical interest, I found it to be quite an intriguing town with its coral houses, carved doors, scattered tombs of long gone souls, a picturesque bay and a simple quiet lifestyle. Evidence of a slave trade long gone is predominate along this section of the coastline, and although fascinating, one couldn't help but feel the pain and suffering many families must have gone through.

The German boma, built in 1895 as a fort and administrative centre, has been completely renovated as a hotel (www.africanadrenalin.com). It is an interesting place to spend an hour or two. Don't forget to purchase a painted coconut brooch made by the local people.

You may also like to visit the prison ruins and the hollow baobab tree that was used to keep unruly prisoners in solitary confinement.

Ten Degrees South

Cell: 0766059380
E-mail: info@tendegreessouth.com
Web: www.tendegreessouth.com

Situated in Mikindani, overlooking the picturesque bay, this renovated 1920 house has rooms that are simple and clean with ceiling fans and mosquito nets.

The guesthouse rooms are US$30.00 per night and the en suite rooms are US$70.00 per night. Since all the rooms are doubles,

German boma before ...

and after

a US$10.00 discount is offered for single occupancy. Both prices include breakfast. Chat to staff for information on diving with ECO2, and attractions in the area.

Diesel costs TSh2 136.00 per litre.

◼ Mikindani to Ruvula

It is approximately 51 kilometres from Mikindani to Ruvula.

Proceed down the coast for 10 kilometres to Mtwara. There is not much of interest in Mtwara. Diesel was available. There's a bank and an ATM that would only take a Visa card. Onions, bread, long-life milk, pineapples, tomatoes, cabbage and beer could be purchased.

From Mtwara, Ruvula is not an easy place to find. The lack of signage and numerous dirt roads make finding your way a challenge.

Stop and ask for directions to the airport road. Once on the right road, take a left at the signpost onto a dirt road. Continue for 6 kilometres to a boom. Entry US$20.00 per person per day and camping costs US$20.00 per person per day.

Move on for a further 11 kilometres and turn left. After 19 kilometres you will pass through a second boom. Continue for a further 5 kilometres and turn right into Ruvula Safaris.

Ruvula Safaris

The campsite overlooks a lovely beach under an abundance of palm trees. Good security. The ablution block is primitive with long drop toilets and cold water. Despite the lack of facilities, we spent four enjoyable days snorkelling and fishing.

Catch of the day!

We discovered that Tunduru has some major ruby and other gemstone mines, guarded by armed guards sitting under trees on the side of the road. At our bush camp that night, Will opened the van bonnet and discovered that rats had made a nest in the foam lining. They were duly evicted!

Ingrid Hardman

Arabic fort built in the early 19th century by the Omani Arabs, on the site of a former Portuguese fort dating from the early 16th century

◼ Ruvula to Kilwa Masoko

It is approximately 312 kilometres from Ruvula to Kilwa Masoko.

This section of road has now been tarred and is in reasonable condition. What took us two days to complete can not be done in four hours! Diesel was available in Kilwa Masoko.

The nearest ATM is in Lindi.

Kilwa Dreams

Cell: 0784585330
E-mail: info@kilwa.co.tz
Web: www.kilwa.co.tz

The main road into Kilwa Masoko runs parallel with the airstrip. At the end of the airstrip take a left turn onto a dirt road that will lead you to Kilwa Dreams.

The campsite, shaded by palm trees, overlooks a beautiful beach. The ablution

ANGEL IN DISGUISE

We arrived at Kilwa Dreams around noon and expressed our desire to visit Kilwa Kisiwani. Patrick, the assistant manager, jumped into action! Despite it being a Sunday and everyone in the sleepy little village was enjoying a day off with their families, Patrick obtained our permit from the District Commissioner, arranged secure parking in the harbour, organised a dhow with a guide and sent us on our way!

Now that is what I call customer care!

facilities were clean with a sit-down toilet but no hot water. There is a bar and small restaurant. Camping costs US$10.00 per person per day.

Kilwa Kisiwani

Kilwa Kisiwani, dating back to the 9th century BC, was once East Africa's most important trading centre. The ruins of the settlement **(right)** are situated on an island a short distance from the mainland and are well worth the visit. The Malindi mosque and cemetery, Kilwa fort, tombs of the Kilwa sultans, the Jangwani mosque and house are just some of the ruins to be explored. US$35.00 per person plus TSh26 000.00 per person entrance fee. Spread out over a wide area, it will take the entire day to get through, so be sure to take plenty of water, lunch, a hat, sunglasses and a good pair of walking shoes. An informative booklet or map can be purchased from the District Commissioner's office.

Visits to this amazing island can be arranged through Kilwa Dreams

The Great Mosque

Arab Tomb

■ Kilwa Masoko to Dar es Salaam

It is approximately 321 kilometres from Kilwa Masoko to Dar es Salaam.

This section of road (B2) was under construction at the time of our passing and a brand-new bridge had been built over the Rufiji River! Diesel was available in Ikwiri.

SHOPRITE – Dar es Salaam

- Tennis Biscuits and Lemon Creams
- 25ml Long-Life Milk
- 500g Kellogg's Corn Flakes
- Yoghurt
- Fuit Juice
- Eggs

Most shops in Tanzania carry the same range of familiar groceries found in South Africa

The B2 north from Kilwa Masoko to Dar es Salaam – now tarred!

Kipepeo Beach Village

Cell: 075426178/0713757515
E-mail: info@kipepeovillage.com
Web: www.kipepeobeach.com
GPS: S06°51.079' E039°21.681'

The Kipepeo Beach Village is situated at Mjimwema, on the south coast of Dar es Salaam, 9 kilometres from the Kigamboni pontoon which links Dar es Salaam to the south coast. The pontoon crosses the harbour mouth, departing from Kivukoni, near the fish market, and arriving in less than 5 minutes at Kigamboni.

Follow the coastal road south for approximately 9 kilometres. Turn left at the signpost and continue for a further kilometre.

Camping Costs US$9.50 per person per day.

KIGAMBONI PONTOON

Operates 24 hours a day.
TSh200.00 per person one way.

Triniti Guest House

Cell: 0769628328
E-mail: triniti.dar@gmail.com
Web: www.triniti.co.za

Situated at 8 Msasani Road, Oysterbay. Quiet area. Close to the slipway. Secure parking. A double room with en-suite costs US$75.00. Breakfast is included.

African fish eagle

ROUTE PLANNING – TANZANIA

DID YOU KNOW?

Zanzibar is a separate state within Tanzania and requires all visitors to have a passport and go through the formalities of customs and immigration.

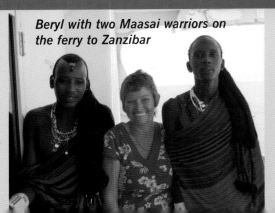

Beryl with two Maasai warriors on the ferry to Zanzibar

Ferry to Zanzibar

Departure time from Dar es Salaam to Zanzibar – 07:00, 09:30, 12:30 and 15:45. Departure time from Zanzibar to Dar es Salaam – 07:00, 09:30, 12:30, and 15:30.

When booking, confirm the above departure times, as they are likely to change without notice, especially on Sundays.

US$35.00 per person
US$25.00 per child under 12
25 kilograms per person permitted

Shades for sale, Zanzibar

The booking office and departure point can be found opposite the Cathedral of St. Joseph, Sokoine Drive, Dar es Salaam.

Booking the ferry to Zanzibar can be a frustrating experience! Every Tom, Dick and Harry is vying for your attention.

We eventually used a tour operator whose office was close to the ferry booking office. A package was designed to meet our requirements and budget. Transport was included for the spice tour, our trip north to Nungwi and to and from the ferry. The booked accommodation was clean and simple with a basic breakfast. At night we went to the Forodhani Gardens, where for a few Tanzanian shillings, you can eat seafood to your heart's content!

You don't have to spend a lot of money in Stone Town if you're quite happy to walk around and look. Local tour operators can make arrangements for you to see other parts of Zanzibar, or you could simply hire a motorbike and go with the wind!

TANZANIA – ROUTE PLANNING

Everyone headed off for a walking tour of ancient Stone Town. After the first alley, about 50 metres from the hotel, we were already lost! Every street looked the same – it was like a huge rabbit warren! We had to put the hotel coordinates into the GPS to find our way back.
Ingrid Hardman

The Forodhani Gardens, Stone Town

Nungwi Beach, northern Zanzibar

■ Dar es Salaam to Tanga

It is approximately 320 kilometres from Dar es Salaam to Tanga.

On leaving Dar es Salaam, we took the A7 west to Chalinze and then the A14 north to Segera. At Segera we took a right turn to Tanga on the A14.

Tanga

Built by the Germans in the late 19th century, Tanga is the second largest seaport and third largest town in Tanzania. Despite that, it remains a pleasant little town with a sleepy semi-colonial atmosphere. There is a small market, situated between Tower and Bank Streets, packed with all sorts of fruit and vegetables. There is also a supermarket overlooking the market on Bank Street, a couple of banks and an Internet café. Diesel was available in Tanga.

Attractions in the area include the Amboni Caves, Galanos Sulphur Springs and the Tongoni Ruins.

PANGANI
In the late 19th century, Pangani had become a terminus for the caravan route from Lake Tanganyika, a major export point for slaves and ivory, and one of the largest ports between Bagamoyo and Mombasa.

I wasn't that enthusiastic about visiting the spice farm but, wow! The guide blew me away with his knowledge of herbs and natural cures. He had about 40 different plants, seeds, leaves, fruits and herbs used to treat any number of ailments. Of course everyone remembered the king and queen of herbs (ginger and nutmeg), considered by the local people to be aphrodisiacs. In his words 'they make fire in the bedroom.' Yeah, right!

Ingrid Hardman

Oloika Sange Beach Bungalows and Campsite

Cell: 0715363636
Web: www.africaguide.com

Follow the A14 from Segera to Tanga. Approximately 34 kilometres from Segera, you will reach Muheza. Take a right turn here and head to Pangani, 42 kilometres to the southeast. Once at Pangani, ask the local people for directions to the ferry, which will take you across the Pangani River. Once on the other side, follow the dirt road for another 40 kilometres. Turn left at the Sange Village sign and proceed to the beach.

This is a fairly new development on the Pangani coast, with a stunning secluded beach and excellent sea views.

Camping costs US$12.00 per person per day.

■ Tanga to Lushoto

It is approximately 164 kilometres from Tanga to Lushoto.

Proceed back to Segera on the A14. At Segera take a right turn to Mombo, on the B1.

Diesel was available at Korogwe.

The road was good tar but watch out for fast trucks and buses that will overtake on a white line and blind rise. Four accidents occurred between Dar es Salaam and Lushoto during our drive.

Oranges, tomatoes, avocados, bananas, coconuts, green peppers, potatoes, carrots and charcoal were for sale en route.

On arrival at Mombo, watch out for the sign to Lushoto, and take a right turn at GPS reading S04°53.286' E038°17.336'. Proceed along a narrow, winding tar road for 34 kilometres. This will take you 1 500 metres up into mist covered mountains, past beautiful waterfalls and fields full of crops.

Diesel was available in Mombo and Lushoto.

Attractions in the area include the magnificent Irente viewpoint and the horned chameleon. You may also wish to visit St. Eugene's Hostel, three kilometres before Lushoto, for homemade cheese and jam. Ask hotel staff for further information.

ANGEL IN DISGUISE

Unable to find any camping facilities in Tanga, we stopped to ask a gentleman if he would advise us on the availability of accommodation in the area. It must have been our lucky day! This gentleman was currently building a campsite at Ushongo Beach in Pangani, approximately 50 kilometres down the coastline, and we were invited to 'pull in' and stay for free. It was an offer we couldn't refuse especially when we hit the beach. What a beautiful spot.

Horned chameleon, Lushoto

The Lawns Hotel

Tel: (027) 2640066
Web: www.lawnshotel.com

Clearly marked as you reach Lushoto. The camping fee was US$12.00 per person per day with a hot water shower. Bar, restaurant, Internet and laundry facilities available. Visa card accepted.

❋ ❋ ❋ ❋ ❋ ❋ ❋ ❋ ❋

The Italian Who Went To Malta

(Must be read with an Italian accent)

One day ima gonna Malta to bigga hotel. Ina morning I go down to eat breakfast. I tella waitress I wanna two pissis toast. She brings me only one piss. I tella her I want to piss. She say go to the toilet. I say you no understand. I wanna to piss onna plate. You sonns ma bitch. I don't even know the lady and she call me sonna ma bitch.

Later I go to eat at the bigga restaurant. The waitress brings me a spoon and a knife but no fock. I tella her I wanna fock. She tell me everyone wanna fock. I tell her you no understand. I wanna fock on the table. She say you better not fock on the table, you sonna ma bitch. So I go back to my room inna hotel and there is no shits onna my bed. Call the manager and tella him I wanna shit. He tell me to go to toilet. I say you no understand. I wanna shit on my bed. He say you better not shit onna bed, you sonna ma bitch.

I go to the checkout and the man at the desk say: " Peace on you ". I say piss on you too, you sonna ma bitch. I gonna back to Italy.

SOUVENIR of MALTA

❋ ❋ ❋ ❋ ❋ ❋ ❋ ❋ ❋

DID YOU KNOW?

The poor digestive system of elephants means that there are lots of nutritious tidbits waiting to be exploited in the dung – something that baboons are particularly adept at doing, especially in winter when food is scarce.

Compliments of the Lawns Hotel!

Early Morning View of Mt. Kilimanjaro

Lushoto to Marangu

It is approximately 252 kilometres from Lushoto to Marangu.

Proceed back to Mombo and take a right turn on to the B1. Continue for 203 kilometres, past Same and Mwanga, to the B1/A23 T-junction. Take a right to Marangu and follow the signposts.

Attractions in the area include hiking Mt. Kilimanjaro, a 104-year-old Catholic Church with beautiful stained glass windows, Lake Chala and the local market. Local guides are available so just ask around.

We were invited to camp at the Marangu Hotel, normally reserved for hikers only, but alternate camping outlets are available in the area.

Try the Coffee Tree Campsite
Cell: 0754691433
GPS: S03°15.509' E037°31.046'.

TANZANIA – ROUTE PLANNING

MOUNT KILIMANJARO

Mt. Kilimanjaro is the highest mountain in Africa at 5 895 metres. It is also the highest free standing mountain in the world. Kilimanjaro is technically not a mountain, but rather a giant stratovolcano that began forming a million years ago when lava spilled from the rift vally zone. While Mt. Kilimanjaro is still covered with ice caps and glaciers at higher levels, global warming is rapidly changing the climate and scientists expect the famed snows of Kilimanjaro to disappear sometime between 2022 and 2033.

■ Marangu to Arusha

It is approximately 127 kilometres from Marangu to Arusha.

Proceed back to the B1/A23 T-junction and continue on to Arusha, via Moshi, on a good tar road. As you approach Arusha, the road will become quite busy and you will need to take a left turn to get into the centre of town, but with so many left turns it can easily become a frustrating experience!

Between the Themi and Goliondoi Rivers, take a left turn onto Simeon Boulevard, past the International Conference Centre and through the traffic circle. At this point Simeon Boulevard will become Goliondoi Road. Continue straight through to the T-junction with Sokoine Road. Take a right turn into Sokoine Road where you should be able to find everything you need.

Diesel cost TSh2 100.00 per litre in Arusha.

Warning!

Two vehicles in our group had the door locks broken and the wheel nuts were stolen off another vehicle that a group member was sitting in! I was hassled in the street for my bread rolls. My husband had to go to the police when a shop owner removed remote control batteries from its packaging after my husband had said they were the wrong size. Unbelievably, the shop owner wanted payment for a sale lost due to the damaged packaging!

You have to have eyes in the back of your head to avoid crime in Arusha. We found a shopping centre in Sokoine Road, with a supermarket (S3°22.511' E36°40.744'), off road parking and good security.

Market Day in Marangu

Arusha National Park

Web: www.tanzaniaparks.com

Clearly signposted as you enter Arusha from Moshi on the A23. It covers 137 sq kilometres and is host to the second highest mountain in Tanzania, Mount Meru (4 562 metres). The park offers excellent game viewing opportunities with the chance to see buffalo, waterbuck, leopard, elephant, yellow baboon, black and white colobus monkey, giraffe and a variety of birds.

Entry US$45.00 per person per day.
Vehicle entry US$40.00 per day.

Camping costs US$30.00 per person per day.

NGORONGORO CRATER

The crater entrance fee is US$200.00 per vehicle per day

BLACK AND WHITE COLOBUS MONKEY

- Unlike other monkeys, the black and white Colobus have no thumbs.
- Newborn Colobuses are completely white.
- Predators include leopard, large eagles and humans.
- Habitat – forest.

TANZANIA – ROUTE PLANNING

DID YOU KNOW?

- The Maasai women build their homes out of wood, straw, ash, dung and mud.
- The Maasai rely on meat, milk and blood for their protein and caloric needs. The blood is taken from a cow and mixed with milk to stop it from coagulating.
- Each Maasai warrior owns three swords: one for training, one for hunting and one for ceremonial purposes.

Arusha to Serengeti National Park and Ngorongoro Crater

From Arusha we made our way west, for roughly 25 kilometres, along the A23 to the Meserani Snake Park and Camp. The entrance to this camp is not easily recognisable, so look out for the bright orange shop on the left with the petrol station across the road from it on the right. The road leading into the Meserani Snake Park and Camp is directly after the petrol station. Diesel costs TSh2 100.00 per litre.

Meserani Snake Park

Cell: 0754440800
E-mail: snakepark@habari.co.tz
              meseranisnakepark@gmail.com
Web: www.meseranisnakepark.com

The campsite offered shade, security, hot water showers, a bar and restaurant. Apart from the interesting snake park and crocodile pen, there is also the Maasai museum and craft centre.

The camp fee is US$8.00 per person and includes a guided tour of the snake park and Maasai Cultural Museum.

THE HIPPOPOTAMUS

- Hippo can only stay under water for about five minutes on a single breath.
- The movement of hippos in water helps to maintain channels threatened by siltation and vegetation growth.
- They live in sociable groups called rafts.
- Hippos do not stamp out fires!

We left our vehicles here while visiting the Serengeti National Park and Ngorongoro Crater.

Serengeti National Park and Ngorongoro Crater

Web: www.tanzaniaparks.com

Visiting the Serengeti National Park and Ngorongoro Crater was one of the highlights of our trip. Unfortunately, it came with a high price tag. After doing a little homework and calling several contacts, we were able to put together a three day, two night all inclusive package for a good price.

ROUTE PLANNING – TANZANIA

Maasai shuka

Displaying male kori bustard

Fun Safaris

Tel: 0754318411
E-mail: fun@habari.co.za
Web: www.fun-safaris.com

Fun Safaris sent a driver/guide called
Livingstone with an eight-seater combi to
pick us up at the Meserani Snake Park.
The package included a day in the
Serengeti National Park and a day in the
Ngorongoro Conservation area. Each night
was spent at a hotel, based within the
park, and included dinner, bed and
breakfast with a boxed lunch. Livingstone
was in constant radio contact with other
drivers so we got to see all the highlights
of the day. We saw a cheetah with two
cubs, a tree-climbing lion, a leopard, zebra
and wildebeest waiting to cross the Mara
River as well as buffalo, elephant and
numerous birds. We doubt we would have
had such an adventurous time had we
been in our own vehicles. The fact that the
group was together made the experience
all the more special.

DID YOU KNOW ...

The suffix *vore* means 'to devour', and
is used to describe an animal by what
it eats.

Animal	Type	Food
Lion	– Carnivore	– meat
Giraffe	– Folivore	– leaves
Hornbill	– Frugivore	– fruits
Elephant	– Granivore	– seeds
Zebra	– Herbivore	– plants
Aardvark	– Insectivore	– insects
Sunbirds	– Nectarivore	– nectar
Fish Eagle	– Piscivore	– fish
Dung Beetle	– Detritivore	– decomposing material

DID YOU KNOW?

The spine in the lumbar region of male
elephants is markedly raised **(below left)**,
whereas that of the female is fairly flat
(below right).

TANZANIA – ROUTE PLANNING

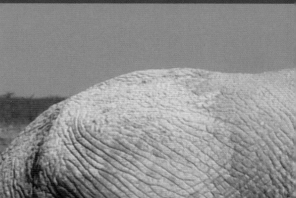

Tree-climbing lion, Serengeti National Park

■ Meserani Snake Park to the Namanga Border Post and Kenya

It is approximately 174 kilometres from the Meserani Snake Park to the Namanga Border Post.

Retrace your steps back towards Arusha on the A23. Just before Arusha you will need to take a left turn to Namanga, the border post between Tanzania and Kenya, which is 149 kilometres away on the A23. This section of road is uneven in places with the odd pothole. Watch out for wandering cattle.

USEFUL WORDS IN SWAHILI

Hello	– Jambo
How are you?	– Habari?
Good/fine	– Nzuri
Thank you	– Asante
Please	– Tafadhali
No	– Hapana
Okay	– Sawa
Sorry	– Samahani

Below: variations in giraffe patterns

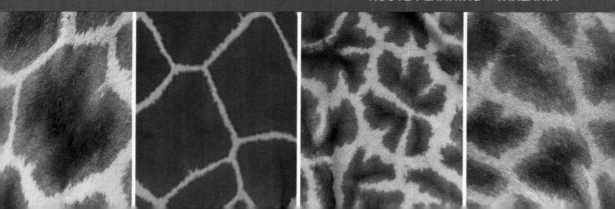

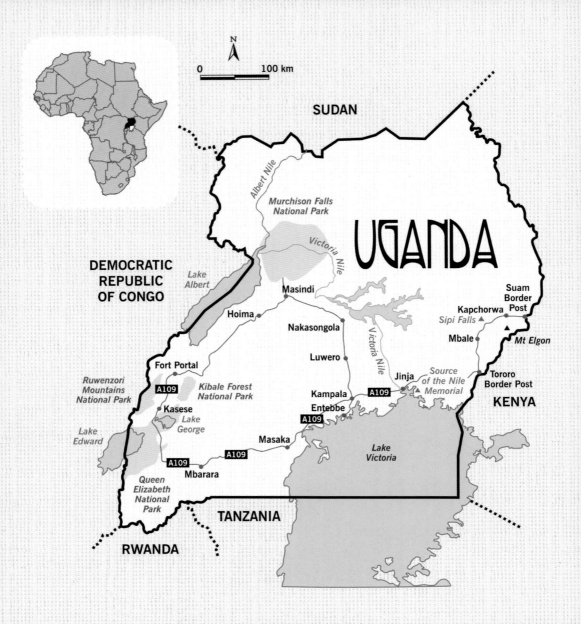

SUDAN

Albert Nile

Murchison Falls
National Park

Victoria Nile

UGANDA

DEMOCRATIC
REPUBLIC
OF CONGO

Lake
Albert

Masindi

Suam
Border
Post

Hoima

Nakasongola

Kapchorwa
Sipi Falls ▲

Mbale
Mt Elgon ▲

Victoria Nile

Luwero

Fort Portal

A109

Ruwenzori
Mountains
National Park

Kibale Forest
National Park

Jinja

Source
of the Nile
▲ Memorial

Tororo
Border Post

Kasese

Lake
George

Kampala

A109

KENYA

Lake
Edward

Entebbe

A109

Masaka

Lake
Victoria

A109
Mbarara

A109

Queen
Elizabeth
National
Park

TANZANIA

RWANDA

0   100 km

N

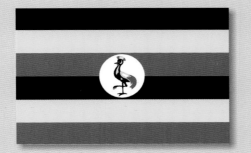

The black stripes symbolise the African people. The yellow symbolises the sun; the red stands for brotherhood and fraternity. The crested crane is a national symbol of Uganda – which was first used during British colonial times. Black, yellow and red were also the colors of the Uganda People's Congress, who came to power in the elections of April 1962.

■ Uganda at a Glance

- Highlights included rafting down the Victoria Nile, visiting the Entebbe Airport, the Uganda Wildlife Education Centre, Murchison Falls National Park, Sipi Falls, Kibale Forest National Park, and the chimpanzees.

- Quick and efficient border posts.

- All money changers at the border post wear yellow T-shirts.

- The main roads are in good condition. Secondary roads not bad. Road signs are readable.

- Diesel and spares readily available.

- Ample banks, ATMs and supermarkets.

- Cadac gas bottles can be refilled in Kampala.

- Kampala is clean and modern with lots to offer.

- The International Hospital in Kampala was clean, efficient and customer orientated.

- Lots of roadside stalls sell a variety of fruit and vegetables.

- Lake Victoria is dirty but the fishing is good.

- Marabou storks everywhere.

- The local people are friendly with a good command of the English language.

- Fillet steak is very cheap in Uganda.

■ General Information

Airlines

South African Airways
Suite 14, Ground Floor, Workers House,
1 Pilkington Road, Kampala
Tel: (041) 4255501
Web: www.flysaa.com

British Airways
Centre Court, 4 Ternan Avenue, Kampala
Tel: (041) 4257414
Web: www.ba.com

Automobile Association

63 Yusuf Road, Kampala
Tel: (041) 4255917
E-mail: aauganda@aau.co.ug
Web: www.aau.co.ug

Border Crossing

Visas are available at all major border posts
and are required by South African passport
holders. A single entry visa is valid for three
months and will cost US$50.00. Extensions
can be arranged through the Immigration
Department in Kampala.

Tel: (041) 4595945/4231031
Web: www.mia.go.ug
www.immigration.go.ug

The road toll fee will be determined by the
distance you plan to cover and length of stay.

Climate

The summer rains fall between September
and November, with daytime temperatures
averaging around 32°C. Dirt roads may
become impassable and mosquitos are more
prevalent. The wnter rains fall between April
and May with daytime temperatures averaging
around 25°C. The sparse vegetation and lack
of water makes this an ideal time to view
game. Chimpanzee tracking is advised
between June and September.

Diplomatic Missions

South Africa
15A Nakasero Road, Kampala
Tel: (041) 4348216/343543
E-mail: kampala.sahc@dirco.gov.za

United Kingdom
4 Windsor Loop, Kampala
Cell: 0312312000
E-mail: Kampala.Bhcinfo@fco.gov.uk

Kenya
41 Nakasero Road, Kampala
Tel: (041) 4258232/5
E-mail: kenyahicom@africaonline.co.ug

Electricity

220/240 volts runnung at 50 Hz. Plugs and sockets may vary but are mostly the British three-square-pin variety.

Medical

Compulsory vaccinations: Yellow Fever.
Recommended vaccinations: Hepatitis A & B, Meningitis, Rabies and Typhoid.
Precautions: Malaria risk.

International Hospital
4686 Barnabas Road, Kampala
Cell: 0312200400

Money

The unit of currency is the Ugandan Shilling (USh). ATMs are usually only available in the larger towns and cities.

Public Holidays

New Year's Day	– January 01
NRM Anniversary Day	– January 26
International Women's Day	– March 08
Easter	– Variable
Labour Day	– May 01
Martyrs' Day	– June 03
Heroes' Day	– June 09
Independence Day	– October 09
Christmas Day	– December 25
Boxing Day	– December 26

Rules of the Road and Vehicle Requirements

Drive on the left-hand side of the road.

Visitors may drive for up to three months on a valid driving license that has been issued in their country of residence.

The speed limit is 50 kilometres per hour in built-up areas and 80 kilometres per hour on the open road. This may vary as per the regulatory traffic signs.

Have your border documents on hand for the numerous police roadblocks.

A fire extinguisher is compulsory if carrying fuel in jerry cans.

The wearing of seat belts is mandatory.

The use of a mobile phone whilst driving is prohibited.

Coffee beans drying in the sun

Service Telephone Numbers and Area Codes

International Code for Uganda: +256

Area codes: Fort Portal 483, Jinja 043, Kabale 486, Kampala 041, Masindi 465, Mbale 045, and Mbarara 485

Ambulance and Police Emergency Service – Tel: 999
Operator – Tel: 0900
Directory Enquiries – Tel: 0901

The Eye Magazine

Web: www.theeye.co.ug

A free insider's guide to Uganda, which contains some useful information on travel, tourism, accommodation, business, shopping and health.

Vehicle Assistance

Fortek (Land Rover specialists)
97/99 Namuwongo Road, Kampala.
Cell: 0772740108
E-mail: service@fortek.ug

Toyota
1 First Street, Kampala.
Cell: 0312301500
E-mail: toyota@toyotaug.co.ug

Residents of the Uganda Wildlife Education Centre

UGANDA – ROUTE PLANNING

We all stopped to buy bread ... which turned out to be gingerbread! Have you ever tried cold meat and tomato on gingerbread?? We also bought chocolate and pistachio ice-cream ... Uganda and Tanzania make the most divine ice-cream.

Ingrid Hardman

Websites and Books for Additional Information

Web: www.i-uganda.com
www.ugandawildlife.org – for current entry fees into the Ugandan National Parks.

'Israel's Lightning Strike – The Raid on Entebbe 1976' by Simon Dustan

'State of Blood: The Inside Story of Idi Amin' by Henry Kyemba

■ Tororo Border Post to Jinja

It is approximately 130 kilometres from the Tororo border post to Explorers Camp.

The border post was friendly, efficient and fairly quick. Having paid a hefty road toll (determined by the route you plan to follow), we naturally assumed the roads in Uganda would be in good nick, so we set off relaxed and ready to enjoy the ride. Boy, were we in for a surprise.

When approaching Jinja from the Tororo border post, you will pass through two traffic circles before crossing over the Owen Falls Dam. At the second traffic circle, before crossing over the dam wall, take a right turn and follow the signs for Bujagali Falls. A left turn will take you into the town of Jinja.

Just before the entry gate to Bujagali Falls, you will see the entrance gate to Explorers Camp on your left.

Diesel was available at the second traffic circle for USh3 200.00 per litre.

Jinja has a lot to offer travellers in the way of banks, supermarkets, guest houses, the Source of the Nile Memorial (USh10 000.00 per person), the Nile Gardens and the Speke Memorial. Well worth a look.

> What is inside a package is known only to its owner.
> **Ugandan Proverb**

We paid US$100.00 in road taxes and expected the road to Jinja to be in fairly good nick ... fat chance! The drivers here are worse than any others we have encountered so far. The tar was a skinny, jagged stretch full of deep potholes and rocky gravel on either side, which was pretty much the only option for us – playing 'chicken an' al'! Dust and the late afternoon sun made visibility extremely difficult and we were continuously squeezed off the road by more aggressive drivers – in a word: it was HELL!! I was completely shattered by the experience. I am not kidding when I say we had a couple of really close shaves with buses and trucks that simply do not give way ... they hog the small section of tar tenaciously! It was rather like an advanced course of dodgem cars and added to that vehicles drive with no lights; bicycles appear out of nowhere and some cyclists whiz by – carrying up to three people! I was convinced we would not make Jinja in one piece. After arriving at Explorers Camp we all gathered around to commiserate on our near death experiences – I kid you not!!!

Explorers Camp

Cell: 0772422373
E-mail: rafting@raftafrica.com
Web: www.raftafrica.com

The campsite grounds have shade but are not that level with patches of bare ground, making the area quite muddy in the rainy season. It is predominately frequented by backpackers and can get quite noisy. The ablution block was not that clean but the view of the Victoria Nile from the shower was beautiful, as there are no back walls! There is a swimming pool and pub where good

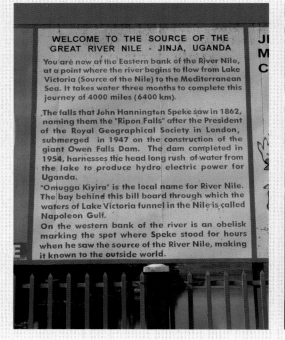

Victoria Nile from Explorers Camp

UGANDA – ROUTE PLANNING

Juma was our guide and he was an absolute hoot with a wicked sense of humour. He first took us through safety precautions and the usual 'if this happens' and tipped us off the boat in calm water to demonstrate how we have to get back on in the rapids. Well, at this point I was ready to go back to camp but that blasted Beryl was determined I saw it through and so I did, muttering much better how I was never going to speak to her again. I survived being flipped out of the raft, trapped under it, shooting numerous rapids and an extremely high waterfall before reaching the end. I was exhausted and I haven't been that scared since jumping out of aeroplanes in my youth.

Ingrid Hardman

inexpensive meals can be ordered. The camping fee was US$7.00 per person. If you would like to go rafting down the Victoria Nile, go to www.raftafrica.com for current prices .

■ Jinja to Kampala

It is approximately 80 kilometres from Jinja to Kampala.

Proceed back to the traffic circle and take a right turn, onto the A109, to Kampala. Good tar road the whole way.

Diesel is available en route. Bread, cabbage, brinjals, pineapple, bananas, potatoes, tomatoes, pumpkin, carrots and pawpaw are for sale at roadside stalls.

As you enter Kampala along the Jinja Road, you will pass the Lugogo Mall on your right, with diesel, ATM facilities, Checkers supermarket and Game store.

While in Kampala, you may wish to take a drive down to Entebbe and visit the Entebbe Airport. It was here in 1976 that the Israelis rescued passengers hijacked by Palestinian terrorists on an Air France airbus. The old airport featured in the film 'The Last King of Scotland' and is currently undergoing renovations. A plaque is to be erected in memory of Dora Bloch (see panel below).

The Uganda Wildlife Education Centre is also worth a visit, especially if you have been unable to see the shoebill stork in the wild.

Entebbe Airport

OPERATION THUNDERBALL/JONATHAN

On July 3, 1976, Israeli paratroopers stormed the Entebbe airport in an attempt to rescue passengers on an Air France airbus that had been hijacked by Palestinian terrorists.

A passenger, 75-year-old Israeli, Dora Bloch, had earlier been rushed to a Ugandan hospital after choking on her food. She was never seen again, presumably murdered by Amin's soldiers.

The only other casualty was Lieutenant Colonel Jonathan Netanyahu. The mission was renamed Operation Jonathan in his memory.

The Israeli paratroopers had pulled off an amazing coup, the reverberations of which spread worldwide.

Red Chilli Hideaway

13 Bukasa Hill View Road,
Butabika, Kampala
Cell: 0772509150
E-mail: reservations@redchillihideaway.com
Web: www.redchillihideaway.com

Although we stayed with friends in Kampala, the Red Chilli Hideaway is well situated and may be worth a look.

◼ Kampala to Murchison Falls National Park

It is approximately 264 kilometres from Kampala to the Murchison Falls National Park.

The tar road north to the Murchison Falls National Park, via Masindi, was in a fairly good condition. This improved when we reached the dirt road north of Nakasongola.

On arrival in Masindi, we made our way through the town to the Masindi Hotel where we had a delicious lunch consisting of Nile Perch, chips and salad.

Stock up on bread and milk at the Shell garage opposite the Masindi Hotel, then take a right turn just before the hotel. The dirt road will take you straight to the Murchison Falls National Park entrance gate.

Diesel was readily available en route. Watch out for motorbikes, bicycles, taxis, buses,

SHOPRITE – Lugogo Mall, Kampala

Whole Chicken	– USh10 900.00
Bokomo Corn Flakes 500g	– USh9 900.00
Hugo's Baked Beans 400g	– USh2 900.00
Ellis Brown Creamer 1kg	– USh32 990.00
Ouma Rusks 500g	– USh12 000.00
Fresh Milk 250ml	– USh2 500.00

Most shops in Uganda carry the same range of familiar groceries found in South Africa.

UGANDA – ROUTE PLANNING

ANGELS IN DISGUISE

Our friends in Kampala were blessed with two amazing employees. Madeleine was the housekeeper and Minessi the driver. When the eight of us arrived, I am sure they must have been tempted to run away, but with a smile on her face Madeleine washed and ironed copious amounts of dirty laundry. She cleaned the house after our late night parties, and prepared breakfast, lunch and supper. Minessi washed weeks of mud off our vehicles, haggled with the locals for better prices, took the guys to the best spares shops, and the ladies on never-ending shopping trips! Despite the sudden increase in their workload they remained polite and helpful with huge smiles on their face. Madeleine and Minessi are truly *Angels in Disguise*.

people and cows! Markets selling a variety of fruit and vegetables were also available en route .

Murchison Falls National Park

Web: www.ugandawildlife.org

Known for its scenic beauty and abundant variety of flora and fauna, this park boasts 76 mammal species including elephants, lion, leopard, buffalo, chimpanzees and 450 bird species, including the rare shoebill stork.

The non-resident entry fee is US$40.00 per person per day. The vehicle entry fee, per vehicle per visit, is US$150.00.

The 50 metre wide Victoria Nile squeezes through a 6 metre wide cleft in the rocks to drop 43 metres. An impressive sight.

A boat trip along the Victoria Nile to the base of the falls will cost US$30.00 per person, and although the view of the falls was stunning, it would be advisable to see it from the top too, at the falls' viewpoint, to really appreciate it.

Game drives, nature walks and fishing are also available.

COLLECTIVE NAMES OF MAMMALS

Buffalo	– Gang, Herd
Cheetah	– Coalition
Elephant	– Parade, Herd
Hyaena	– Clan
Impala	– Rank
Jackal	– Skulk
Leopard	– Leap
Lion	– Pride, Sault, Sowse
Warthog	– Sounder
Wild Dog	– Pack
Wildebeest	– Herd, Implausibility
Zebra	– Dazzle, Zeal, Cohort

There is a basic campsite on the banks of the Victoria Nile, at the falls' viewpoint. Although the facilities were poor, there was plenty of shade, a basic shower cubicle, water, pristine bush and stunning views of the river with no noisy backpackers. Camping costs USh15 000.00 per person and there is no charge to see the falls from the viewpoint. The campsite is clearly signposted from the main dirt road.

The ferry crossing over the Victoria Nile, to view game, will cost USh20 000.00 for the vehicle and USh5 000.00 for each passenger.

Warning – there are tsetse flies in the area.

It was a short drive to the top of the falls. What a sight! It was absolutely fantastic! The wide Nile River with its boiling cauldrons of water is suddenly squashed into a narrow cleft, about four metres wide, and the crashing turns into cascading torrents to the bottom. The view from the top is so different … it was breathtakingly scary!

Ingrid Hardman

Murchison Falls

Thunder is not yet rain.

Only a dead fish goes with the flow.

African Proverbs

Red Chilli Rest Camp

Cell: 0772509150
Web: www.redchillihideaway.com

Situated in the park, this campsite had very little shade and grass with a whole lot of devil thorns, mosquitoes and noisy backpackers. However, it did have a pleasant bar that served good basic meals. The camping fee was US$7.00 per person per day.

■ Murchison Falls National Park to the Amabere Caves

It is approximately 348 kilometres from the Murchison Falls National Park to the Amabere Caves.

Retrace your steps back to the Masindi Hotel 76 kilometres away. At the T-junction turn right onto a dirt road to Hoima (about 56 kilometres away). This road deteriorates as you approach the town. Pass through Hoima and make your way to Fort Portal, 204 kilometres down the road.

Once at Fort Portal you will pass through two traffic circles. Take a right turn at the second traffic circle and continue for approximately 9 kilometres to the Amabere Caves, signposted on the right.

There is a supermarket (Andrew's Supermarket) on the right, after passing through the first traffic circle. There is also a Standard Bank.

Diesel was available in Hoima and Fort Portal. Tomatoes, mangoes, cabbage, pawpaw and bundles of wood were also available en route.

Masindi Hotel

MURCHISON FALLS:

It was here in 1954, that the American writer Ernest Hemingway and his wife Mary Welsh, arrived after their chartered Cessna had dipped to avoid hitting a flock of birds, in the process clipping a wing on an abandoned telegraph wire, and forcing a crash landing in which Hemingway dislocated his right shoulder and Mary cracked several ribs. The following day, Hemingway chartered a Da Haviland to take them to Entebbe. However, on take off the plane crashed and burst into flames. Although Hemingway survived, the extent of his injuries resulted in his gradual decline and death by suicide in 1961.

Amabere Caves

The campsite here is in a private garden with ample shade, green grass, flowers and hot water showers. In other words: a traveller's dream accommodation! This is a great spot to relax, catch up on laundry, and explore the caves and crater lakes. There is a small lounge area and bar where basic meals can be ordered. Camping costs USh20 000.00 per couple per day and US$5.00 per couple to visit the caves.

■ Amabere Caves to the Kibale Forest National Park

It is approximately 43 kilometres from the Amabere caves to Kibale Forest National Park.

Retrace your steps back to Fort Portal. At the traffic circle turn left. Pass through the town and the second traffic circle. Continue straight as if heading back to Hoima.

Immediately before the bridge over the Mpanga River, take a right turn onto a good dirt road. After 500 metres you will pass a hospital on your right. Continue for roughly 12 kilometres, then take a left turn. A further 11 kilometres will take you to the Kibale Forest National Park.

Kibale Forest National Park

Web: www.ugandawildlife.org

Kibale Forest National Park is a lush tropical rainforest with one of the highest diversity and density of primates in Africa today, tallying 13 species. These include the endangered chimpanzee **(right)**, the black and white colobus, the blue monkey, the grey-cheeked mangabey and the red colobus.

There are over 325 species of birds, over 250 different tree species, a colourful variety of butterflies **(below)** and a number of impressive mammals including the forest elephant, bush pig and duiker.

The non-resident fee for entry into the park is US$40.00 per person per day. The vehicle entry fee is US$150.00.

ROUTE PLANNING – UGANDA

We were all beginning to worry that they would be as elusive as the shoebill stork, but then we heard their calls. Shortly after, a lone male crossed the path in front of us. I was taken aback as to how big and black they are and how long their hair is. Then the whole troop was there: in the trees, on the ground, grooming, scratching and nibbling leaves. I was completely unprepared for the effect the chimps had on me! It was as if I had had a sneak preview into a different world – an ancient primitive world. They are so incredibly human-like. No wonder Jane Goodall loved them so passionately. What a wonderful experience. I feel very privileged to have spent time with them.

Ingrid Hardman

Guided Forest Walks

The most popular guided forest walk is to see the chimpanzees. This departs from Kanyanchu at a cost of US$150.00 per person. We were fortunate enough to find a troop of approximately 20 chimpanzees (with the alpha male) on the forest floor grooming, playing and searching for tidbits. This was amazing and well worth the visit.

Don't forget to take a waterproof cover for your camera and video.

It would also be advisable to wear long pants, tucked into your socks, and boots to avoid the bite of safari ants commonly found in forest areas.

Kanyanchu River Camp

The campsite is very basic. It is literally a huge field surrounded by the forest. There is plenty of green grass with some shade and the ablution block is a short walk away. The night sounds here are amazing.

Camping costs USh15 000.00 per person per day.

THE PUTZI FLY

The putzi fly likes to lay its eggs, often undetected, on laundry drying in the sun. If the clothing is not ironed or left for 48 hours before wearing, the eggs will hatch and the larvae will burrow under the skin, causing a painful boil-like sore. DO NOT SQUEEZE IT. If it is a putsi fly you will see a black dot in the centre of the boil that wiggles when touched. With a sterilized pin or needle, gently lift the top of the boil and insert a drop of alcohol. This should encourage the worm to surface for air. Use gentle pressure to help remove the worm – in one piece. Beware: a broken worm can cause a serious infection. Once completed, clean the area well, apply an antiseptic cream and cover with a plaster.

One couple in our group washed their sheets at the Kanyanchu campsite. Once dry, they put them straight back onto their rooftop tent mattress and subsequently broke out in numerous boils, extracting between 30–40 worms each! You have been warned!

SAFARI ANTS

Safari ants swarm about in savannah and forest areas at the start of the rains. Their bite is ferocious and they often attack in large numbers. Always check the campsite before setting up camp and tuck your pants into your socks when out walking.

Eastern Grey Plantation Eater

■ Kibale Forest National Park to the Ruwenzori Mountains National Park

It is approximately 120 kilometres from Kibale Forest National Park to the Ruwenzori Mountains National Park.

Make your way back to Fort Portal. Take the Fort Portal/Kasese Road (A109) for 100 kilometres, on good tar. At Mubuku, take a right after the bridge and follow the dirt road to Nyakalengija. This is the point from which all hiking begins.

There was a large variety of fruit and vegetables for sale en route, including tomatoes, cabbage, pineapple, onions, pawpaw, bananas and potatoes.

ROUTE PLANNING – UGANDA

THE GLACIERS

All six of the highest mountains – Stanley, Speke, Baker, Emin, Gesi and Luigi – had glaciers. By 2001, the glaciers on the first three mountains had greatly reduced and the last three have completely melted. Some areas that were covered with snow are now bare rock – taken from the Bakonzo Booklet on the *History and Culture in the Ruwenzori Mountains of the Moon.*

Ruwenzori Mountains National Park

Web: www.ugandawildlife.org
www.mountainruwenzorinationalparkuganda.com

The Ruwenzori Mountains are the highest mountain range in Africa and lie on the western side of Uganda, between Lake Albert and Lake Edward and along the Democratic Republic of Congo border. A good 120 kilometres long and 48 kilometres wide, these mountains were created during the formation of the Great Rift Valley. They were first declared a forest reserve in 1941 and then a national park in 1991. In 1995 they became a World Heritage Site. Capped with ice and snow, this magnificent mountain range supports amazing vegetation and spectacular scenic beauty. It is known primarily for its challenging hiking and climbing possibilities but also includes 177 bird species, an assortment of mammals and a colourful variety of butterflies.

> If I have ever seen magic,
> it has been in Africa.
>
> – John Hemingway

Tour Holiday Inn Accommodation

Situated along the dirt road to Nyakalengija in the village of Ibanda.

They offer clean, well maintained rooms, a dining room for meals and excellent security.

The owners were very accommodating and allowed us to camp on their back lawn. A single room costs US$45.00 and a double room costs US$65.00. Breakfast is included.

There is also a Tour Holiday Inn in Kasese.

■ Ruwenzori Mountains National Park to the Queen Elizabeth National Park

It is approximately 65 kilometres from the Ruwenzori Mountains National Park to the Queen Elizabeth National Park.

Make your way back to the main road (A109). Take a right onto good tar and head for Kasese, 8 kilometres down the road where diesel is available.

UGANDA – ROUTE PLANNING

Patas Monkey

THE ORIGIN OF MAMMAL NAMES

Buffalo

From the Portuguese name 'bufalo'

Bushbuck

Derived from the habitat it prefers

Caracal

From the Turkish name 'garah-gulak' meaning black ear

Cheetah

From the Hindu word Chita meaning 'spotted one'

Giraffe

From the Arabic word 'xirapha' meaning 'one who walks swiftly'

Leopard

From the Greek words 'pardus' for panther and 'leon' for lion

Zebra

Italian or Portuguese name given to the species in the Congo region

Vehicle parts may be purchased on Margarita Road next to the Shell garage.

Proceed through Kasese and continue for 38 kilometres. Take a right at the signpost and proceed to the Katunguru entrance gate 9 kilometres down a dirt road. Once registered, proceed for a further 21 kilometres to the campsite at Mweya.

Queen Elizabeth National Park

Web: www.ugandawildlife.org

The Queen Elizabeth National Park is Uganda's most popular park and is situated along the eastern shore of Lake Edward in western Uganda.

The 1 978 sq kilometre park is composed primarily of savannah, areas of swamp and dense cover of acacia and euphorbia trees. Ninety-five mammal species have been recorded with around 20 predators. We were fortunate enough to see a young male leopard and two giant forest hogs.

The Mweya campsite is not the best of camps with minimal shade, patches of grass, a resident marabou stork, hippo and

Marabou storks ... they look like pterodactyls flying over us and landing in the campsite to forage in the bins! I have decided that these birds are my favourite. They look for all the world like bored butlers. Their thick bills look like enormous tweezers and they really are the most revolting looking birds, yet strangely appealing! We had a good laugh when one spotted the Kotzes' fillet steak thawing on the bonnet and almost got away with it!

Ingrid Hardman

warthog. However, there is a grassed pergola and a pretty view over Lake Edward. The ablution block is basic with cold water.

There are more appealing private campsites situated along the Kazinga Channel, but there are no facilities available.

To get to Ishasha, the southernmost camp in the park, proceed back to the main road, turn right and continue for approximately 4 kilometres then take a right turn to Ishasha, roughly 70 kilometres along a dirt road. This area is commonly known for its tree-climbing lions. The campsite is tucked away in a grove of shady trees with lovely green grass overlooking a small river. Unfortunately, there are no facilities.

The non-resident fee for entry into the park is US$40.00 per person per day. The vehicle entry fee, per vehicle per visit, is US$150.00. Camping costs USh15,000.00 per person per day.

From here, we made our way back to Kampala via the town of Mbarara, where bank facilities and diesel can be found.

UGANDA – ROUTE PLANNING

Before going out with a widow, first find out how her husband died!

African Proverb

Sacred Ibis

...unt Elgon

ROUTE PLANNING – UGANDA

The scenery along the way was breathtaking.
Each mountainside was a patchwork quilt of
green crops. Every centimetre was utilised –
from the valleys to the very tip of the
mountains at 60 to 70 degree angles.

Ingrid Hardman

COULOURFUL TRADE NAMES

- Be Clean Dry Cleaners
- Green Hands Beauty Salon
- Hair Salon and Barbar

■ Kampala to Jinja

Ripe jackfruit

It is approximately 80 kilometres from Kampala to Jinja.

We retraced our steps back to Jinja, but this time we stayed at the Eden Rock Resort, across the road from Explorers Camp. Entry is via the Bujagali Falls entrance gate. To avoid the entrance fee, let the guard know you will only be camping.

Eden Rock Resort

Tel: (043) 4131476
E-mail: contact@edenrocknile.com
Web: www.edenrocknile.com

Despite reports in the Bradt travel guide on Uganda, our stay here was quite pleasant and a definite improvement on Explorers Camp. The campground was level grass with ample shade and a view of the Victoria Nile. The new ablution block was clean with hot water. Meals are available and we did not experience any noise from the bar. Camping costs US$5.00 per person per day.

UGANDA – ROUTE PLANNING

Saturday, June 09, 2007 – In today's newspaper there is coincidently an article on Idi Amin. It suggests that he was not the murderous dictator he was perceived to be and that Israel masterminded the hijacking in order to discredit Arafat in the eyes of the USA! Oh, well, that's debatable!

Ingrid Hardman

■ Jinja to Sipi Falls

It is approximately 214 kilometres from Jinja to Sipi Falls.

Retrace your steps back to the traffic circle and turn left as if heading back to the Tororo border post. 39 kilometres down the road you will reach Iganga. Diesel and banking facilities were available in Iganga.

Continue for a further 11 kilometres then take a left to Mbale on a good tar road. Some 98 kilometres later you will pass through the centre of Mbale to the traffic circle with the clock tower in the middle. Continue straight for approximately 8 kilometres. Take a right turn at the signpost reading 'Sislyi Falls 30 kilometres.'

Continue straight to Kapchorwa. Approximately 52 kilometres later you should reach the Twilight Guest House, signposted on the left-hand side of a corner bend in the road.

Sipi Falls from the campsite at Twilight Guest House

Mount Elgon is really beautiful. Reminiscent of the Mpumalanga, Transkei and Lesotho all rolled into one. It is studded with numerous waterfalls and thick forested gorges. Sipi Falls is the most spectacular of all.

Ingrid Hardman

Sipi Falls

The Sipi River cascades down the slopes of Mount Elgon, over a series of four waterfalls, to the foothills below. The largest of these waterfalls, with a 99 metre drop, can clearly be seen from the Twilight Guest House.

Twilight Guest House

Cell: 0772625199
E-mail: twilightsipicampsite@yahoo.co.ug
Web: www.twilightsipicampsite.com

This was a fairly new guest house so their camp area was not that level. It had patches of mud and very little shade. However, the view over the falls was spectacular. The ablution block was clean with loads of lovely hot water. Camping costs US$10.00 per person per day. A guided walk to the falls can be arranged.

■ Sipi Falls to the Suam Border Post and Kenya

It is approximately 93 kilometres from Sipi Falls to the Suam Border Post.

Although we were advised by the South African Embassy to avoid the Sipi Falls/ Mt Elgon area, we felt it would be far safer than chancing our luck on the bad road back to the Tororo border post! As it was, the locals were very friendly and we didn't experience any problems. However, I would not suggest you follow this route in the rainy season.

From the Twilight Guest House, we took a left back onto the main road to the Suam border post, via Kapchorwa. The view over the lowlands was beautiful with lots of waterfalls en route. The road climbs quite high and some sections are in bad need of repair. On one section the whole village, women and children included, were out fixing the road. I felt bad driving over their hard work.

The Suam border post is open from 06:00 to 18:00 daily but will happily accommodate travellers at any time of the day or night. Although pleasant, quick and efficient, they were not too familiar with the Carnet de Passage. You will be required to submit your road toll receipt before departure.

USEFUL WORDS IN LUGANDA

Hi	– Ki kati
Good morning	– Wasuze otya
Please	– Mwattu
Thank you	– Weebale
Sorry	– Nsonyiwa

Shoebill stork

At the Suam border post we encountered a 'nutcase.' This one began by praising and blessing us, but then turned nasty when we refused to give him a soda drink! He then proceeded to remove all the valve caps from the tyres. Eventually, the Ugandan police chased him and retrieved them for us!

Ingrid Hardman

KENYA – ROUTE PLANNING

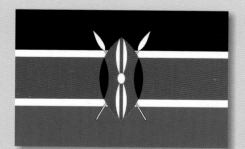

The flag of Kenya was adopted on December 12, 1963, and is based on the flag of KANU (Kenya African National Union). The black colour symbolises black majority, the red colour is for the blood shed during the struggle for freedom, and the green colour for natural wealth. The white fimbriation was added later and symbolises peace.

The defence of freedom is symbolised by a traditional Maasai shield and two spears.

■ Kenya at a Glance

- Highlights included the Kakamega Forest National Park, Masai Mara National Reserve, Lake Magadi, Gede Ruins, Lamu Island, Samburu National Reserve, Lake Turkana and of course the beaches.

- Tourist attractions in Kenya have a three-tier pricing system with different prices for local residents, East African residents and foreigners. Needless to say, foreigners pay the highest price. As a result, we refused to visit some of Kenya's attractions due to the expense.

- The bulk of Kenya's roads are in a bad state. Bus and truck drivers are a law unto themselves and a danger to fellow road users.

- Road signs in Kenya are few and far between. Should you find one it's generally rusted and impossible to read.

- Fuel is readily available throughout Kenya except for the northern regions where fuel stations tend to be miles apart.

- The people of Kenya are very friendly and we did not experience any crime.

- Fruit and vegetables are available from local village markets and on the side of the road.

- Most accommodation along the coast is closed mid-year due to the trade winds and copious amount of seaweed washed ashore.

- Street parking must be paid for and the receipt displayed on the vehicle window. The fee paid is valid for one day in the town of origin only!

- A parked tourist vehicle, with passengers inside, will attract a dozen or more 'salesmen' determined to make a sale no matter how many times you say, 'No, thank you!'

- Nairobi is clean, safe and a pleasure to walk around in.

- Lamu Island is a mini version of Zanzibar without the tourists.

- The closer you get to western Kenya and Lake Victoria, the harder it is to find accommodation. However, chat to the local farmers as most of them are only too happy to let you set up camp on their land.

- Of all the countries we visited, Kenya showed the most severe signs of soil erosion and land degradation.

ROUTE PLANNING – KENYA

The A104 west to Uganda was under construction, but the new road should be up and running by now.

- If you think the speed humps in South Africa are bad, then wait till you get to Kenya! They are humungous, unpainted and come with no warning signs. You don't slow down for these humps, you stop!

- Good range of beer!

◼ General Information

Airlines

South African Airways
International House,
Mama Ngina Street, Nairobi
Tel: (020) 2247342/2217437

British Airways
The Citadel, Muthithi Road, Westlands
Tel: (020) 6980000

Automobile Association of Kenya

Airport North Road, off Mombasa Road, Nairobi
Tel: (020) 2612300/11
Web: www.aakenya.co.ke

Samburu woman

DID YOU KNOW?

- The Samburu tribe is closely related to the Maasai and speak the same language.

- Samburu warriors paste their hair with red ochre to create a visor to shield their eyes from the sun.

- Samburu families live in a group of huts made of branches, mud and dung, surrounded by a fence made of thorn bushes.

Border Crossing

Foreign permit: US$100.00
(valid for three months)

Visas are available for purchase at the border post. South African passport holders do not require a visa to enter Kenya if staying for less than 30 days. A three month visa will cost US$50.00 and is valid from the time of entry.
Web: www.kenya.org.za
www.homeaffairs.go.ke

Climate

The summer rains fall between November and March with daytime temperatures averaging around 34°C. Temperatures in northern Kenya will be a lot higher and precautions need to be taken against sunburn and dehydration. The cooler winter season experiences light rainfall and runs between June and October. Night time temperatures can drop as low as 5°C. Most accommodation along the coast is closed mid-year due to the trade winds and copious amount of seaweed washed ashore.

Diplomatic Missions

South Africa
Roshanmaer Place, Lenana Road, Nairobi
Tel: (020) 2827100
E-mail: sahcadmin@africaonline.co.ke

United Kingdom
Upper Hill Road, Nairobi
Tel: (020) 2873000/2844000
E-mail: Nairobi.Enquiries@fco.gov.uk

Ethiopia
State House Avenue, Nairobi
Tel: (020) 2732050/2
E-mail: info@ethioembnairobi.org
Web: www.ethioembnairobi.org

Electricity

220/240 volts AC with a three-square-pin and two-pin plug.

Kenya Tourism Guide

This useful guide, found in supermarkets, contains a variety of maps on the main towns and information on tourist attractions, accommodation, banking facilities and much more.

ROUTE PLANNING – KENYA

We had the usual haggling at the border post but it went fairly quickly and smoothly … it's only the locals trying to sell currency on the black market, and trinkets, even forcing bangles onto your arms. Others try to sell vehicle stickers that they claim are necessary for driving in Kenya. A con for sure!

Ingrid Hardman

Medical

Compulsory vaccinations: Yellow Fever.
Recommended vaccinations: Cholera,
Hepatitis A & B, Meningitis, Tetanus, Typhoid.
Precautions: Malaria risk.

Upper Hill Medical Centre
Ralph Bunche Road, Nairobi
Tel: (020) 2721580

Emergency Medical Flights
Tel: +44 (0) 8450552828

Money

The unit of currency is the Kenyan Shilling (KSh).

ATMs are available in the larger towns and cities.

Public Holidays

New Year's Day	– January 01
Easter	– Variable
Labour Day	– May 01
Madaraka Day	– June 01
Moi Day	– October 10
Kenyatta Day	– October 20
Independence Day	– December 12
Christmas Day	– December 25
Boxing Day	– December 26

Rules of the Road and Vehicle Requirements

Drive on the left-hand side of the road.

Visitors may drive for up to three months on a valid driving license that has been issued in their country of residence.

The wearing of seatbelts is mandatory.

The speed limit is 50 kilometres per hour in built-up areas and 110 kilometres per hour on the open road. This may vary as per the regulatory traffic signs.

ZA sticker is required.

A fire extinguisher is compulsory if carrying fuel in jerry cans.

Service Telephone Numbers and Area Codes

International Code for Kenya: +254

Area Codes: Diani 012, Eldoret 053, Garissa 046, Kakamega 056, Kilifi 012, Lamu 012, Malindi 042, Marsabit 069, Mombasa 041, Nairobi 020, Nanyuki 062, Niavasha 050.

Ambulance and Police Emergency Service –
Tel: 999
Operator – Tel: 0196
Directory Enquiries – Tel: 0991

KENYA – ROUTE PLANNING

Chalbi Desert, northern Kenya

Smart Card System

Web: www.kws.go.ke

This is a rechargeable electronic card, issued by the Kenya Wildlife Service (KWS), for the payment of entrance fees on entering those parks where it is implemented. For example: Aberdare National Park, Amboseli National Park, Lake Nakuru National Park, Nairobi National Park and the Tsavo National Reserve.

Cards may be obtained from a point of issue (POI) and a stipulated amount of money may be deposited at the same time, but be warned: money deposited and not used is not refundable!

Further deposits can be made at any point of sale (POS).

Vehicle Assistance

Land Rover Kenya
Lusaka/Bunyaia Road, Nairobi
Tel: (020) 653098/650795
E-mail: info@cmcmotors.com
Web: www.cmcmotors.com

Toyota
Uhuru Highway/Lusaka Road, Nairobi
Tel: (020) 6767000
E-mail: enquiries@toyotakenya.com

Websites and Books for Additional Information

Web: www.kws.go.ke
www.traveldiscoverkenya.com
www.magicalkenya.com
www.kenyalogy.com

'Out of Africa' by Karen Blixen
'Born Free' by Joy Adamson
'The Man-Eaters of Tsavo' by John Henry Patterson

Vulturine guineafowl

Life is the best gift; the rest is extra.

Swahili Proverb

■ Namanga Border Post to Nairobi

It is approximately 165 kilometres from the Namanga border post to Nairobi.

Proceed along the A104 for roughly 135 kilometres to the T-junction with the A109 Nairobi/Mombasa road. Take a left turn to Nairobi (approximately 30 kilometres away). Watch out for wandering cattle and potholes along this section of road. It would be advisable not to enter Nairobi during peak traffic times unless you are prepared to wait in a never-ending queue with impatient motorists constantly pushing in from every conceivable angle.

The city has changed considerably and no longer deserves the name 'Nairobbery.' The streets were clean and free of street traders and rubbish. The traffic circles, gardens and parks were neatly maintained and a day spent wandering around the city was harassment-free. Thank you, Nairobi. It was a pleasure to visit.

Sunday afternoon traffic heading into Nairobi. Bit of a bummer for those travelling in the opposite direction!

Diesel was available along this stretch of road and ranged in price from KSh83.10 to KSh93.60 per litre.

Due to our early arrival in Nairobi we decided to push on to Lake Naivasha. However, for those of you who would like to stay over, there are several campsites close to the city.

KENYA – ROUTE PLANNING

Mix a little paraffin in water and spray the mixture around the camp to keep ants, snakes and other creepy crawlies out!

Wildebeest Eco Camp

Cell: 0734770733
E-mail: info@wildebeesttravels.com
Web: www.wildebeestecocamp.com

On entering Nairobi, the A109 becomes the A104. As you enter the city centre, the A104 becomes the Uhuru Highway. Once on the Uhuru Highway, turn left into Langata Road and then right into Mokoyeti Road West, to number 151.

This camp is well situated with easy access into Nairobi and the main road leading east and west. It is also in close proximity to the huge Nakumatt Superstore and Land Rover Kenya. Camping costs US$7.00 per person.

MATATU

A minibus with an ear-piercing sound system and an unlimited carrying capacity with two speeds – stationary or flat out!

KANGA

- A colourful garment worn by women throughout eastern Africa.

- It is a rectangular piece of cotton fabric, often with a border along all four sides (pindo), a central part (mji) and a message (jina or ujumbe).

- Kangas are all about communicating a message – usually in the form of riddles, metaphors, a poetic phrase or proverb.

- They are a valuable medium of expressing personal, political, social and religious ideas and aspirations.

- Apart from being used as shawls, skirts and headscarfs, kangas are also used as curtains, tablecloths and prayer mats.

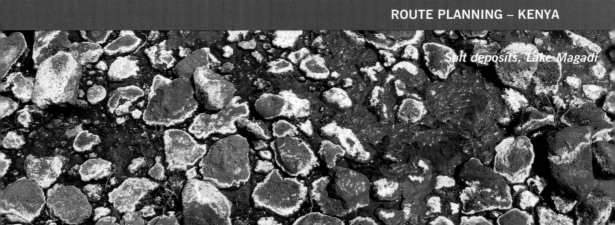

Salt deposits, Lake Magadi

Nairobi to Lake Naivasha

It is approximately 85 kilometres from Nairobi to Lake Naivasha.

Take the Uhuru Highway (A104) west to Naivasha. Once there, you will need to cross over the railway line to get to the Moi South Lake Road. Due to major construction, a network of detours and a lack of road signs at the time of our visit, I am unable to give specific directions, so stop and ask if you are unsure of where to go.

Fisherman's Camp

Cell: 0718880634
E-mail: fishermanscamp@gmail.com
Web: www.fishermanscamp.com

Situated several kilometres down the Moi South Lake Road, this camp offers lovely green grass, shade, clean ablutions and direct access to Lake Naivasha with a beautiful variety of birdlife. There is also a bar and restaurant. Camping costs KSh700.00 per person per day.

Masaai necklaces

KENYA – ROUTE PLANNING

Each country has its own beer brand ... Mosi, Club, Kilimanjaro, Bells, Nile Special, Kutchi Kutchi etc. ... and all the bottles are identical. If you take your empty bottle of Mosi from Zambia to a store in Tanzania, it won't be accepted! So the cunning plan was to soak the labels off and voilà ... they take them back! That's my tailpiece for the day!

Ingrid Hardman

Attractions in the area include the Elsamere Conservation Centre (former home of the late Joy Adamsom of 'Born Free' fame), Hells Gate National Park and the Elementeita Weavers (GPS S00°46.759' E036°25.314').

Lake Naivasha to Kakamega Forest National Park

It is approximately 265 to 300 kilometres from Lake Naivasha to Kakamega Forest National Park.

Once back on the A104, continue west towards the town of Gilgil 24 kilometres away. This section of the A104, all the way through to the border with Uganda, was under construction at the time of our visit so distances quoted may no longer be reliable.

Between Gilgil and Nakuru, 38 kilometres away, is Lake Elmenteita.

Diesel was available in Nakuru. Banking facilities and a supermarket were also available.

Continue along the A104 for approximately 103 kilometres. At this point, take a left turn onto the C36 to Kapsabet from where the C36 will become the C39. Proceed to the T-junction with the A1, roughly 93 kilometres away. Take a right turn onto the A1 and continue for 34 kilometres to the town of Kakamega. Diesel was available and there was a huge daily market selling a variety of fruit and vegetables, a supermarket and Barclays Bank with ATM facilities.

Approximately 15 kilometres north of Kakamega you will find the entrance gate to Kakamega Forest National Park on your right.

Lake Naivasha

Lake Elmenteita

Lake Elmenteita

This is a beautiful lake, surrounded by mountains, with a large gathering of flamingoes. There is also a hot spring at the eastern end of the lake, within easy walking distance (S00°28.348' E36°15.515'). Entry is KSh600.00 per vehicle which goes towards community projects.

KENYA – ROUTE PLANNING

SCHOOL MOTTOES

- Work Hard for Success
- Rise and Shine
- Striving for Excellence
- Bright Future for All
- Shaping the Future Today
- Strive to Thrive

Crying Stone of Ilesi

CRYING STONE OF ILESI

Situated on the right-hand side of the road, 6 kilometres before entering the town of Kakamega. It consists of a large round boulder balanced on top of an 8 metre high column of rock with water somehow constantly flowing down a groove in the middle. The local community will gladly guide you to the site for an exorbitant fee. If like us you aren't prepared to be ripped off, the view from the road is just as good.

Kakamega Forest National Park

Web: www.kws.go.ke

The last remaining natural forest in Kenya. It is hard to imagine that all of Kenya once looked like this. It gives one new respect for Livingstone and his crew making their way through the thick bush of an Africa we never knew.

Entry US$25.00 per person per day, KSh35 000.00 per vehicle per day and camping costs US$15.00 per person per day. The entrance gate is open from 06:00 to 18:00 daily.

Although expensive, the forest is a beautiful place teeming with all sorts of bugs, butterflies, birds and wildlife. The campsite is a clearing in the forest with a long drop toilet and cold water shower. There is a thatched rondavel for cooking and shelter from the rain.

A guided walk (KSh500.00 per person) through the forest is a must. Be sure to ask for Solomon, who has a unique ability to mimic bird calls and a wealth of information on the forest and its inhabitants. With 400 butterfly species, 330 bird species, 20 snake species, the rare de brazza's monkey, the red-tailed monkey, black and white colobus monkey, the blue monkey, hammer-headed fruit bat and the flying squirrel, there is plenty to see and do.

Kakamega Forest

KENYA – ROUTE PLANNING

It was great! Within the first hour we had seen four different species of primates, numerous birds and hundreds of butterflies!

Ingrid Hardman

Kakamega Forest National Park to the Malaba Border Post and Uganda

It is approximately 102 kilometres from Kakamega Forest National Park to the Malaba border post.

Head north along the A1 to the town of Webuye, approximately 30 kilometres away. Take a left turn onto the A104 and head for the border post at Malaba.

Our entry point back into Kenya was via the Suam border post at the base of Mount Elgon.

I know it's around here somewhere!

Suam Border Post to the Chorlim Wildlife Sanctuary

It is approximately 30 kilometres from the Suam border post to the Chorlim Wildlife Sanctuary.

Continue along the dirt road, for roughly 9 kilometres, to the tar road. Take a right turn and then first left onto another dirt road. Proceed for 4 kilometres before you turn right at the sign for Mount Elgon Lodge. Chorlim Wildlife Sanctuary is a few metres further down the road and easily recognisable by its black and white striped painted gates.

Diesel was available after the border post and cabbages, bananas, oranges and tomatoes were for sale en route.

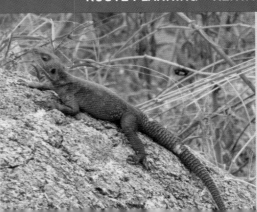

Chorlim Wildlife Sanctuary

Web: www.murembaretreatkitale@gmail.com

This is a lovely campsite in amongst the bush with lots of green grass and shade. Clean ablution block with hot water. For KSh400.00 per person, you can walk amongst the rhino, zebra, giraffe and eland with the opportunity to hand feed the eland and the giraffe! Camping costs US$12.00 per person per day.

◾ Chorlim Wildlife Sanctuary to Lake Bogoria via the Cherangani Hills

Via the Cherangani Hills, it is approximately 354 kilometres from Chorlim Wildlife Sanctuary to Lake Bogoria.

On leaving the Chorlim Wildlife Sanctuary, take a right turn onto a good dirt road. After a couple of metres you will come to a four-way stop. Continue for roughly 9 kilometres until you reach a T-junction,

Village high up in the Cherangani Hills

KENYA – ROUTE PLANNING

Brian spoke to the local men and before long they were happily posing for photographs and one was hired to guard our camp that night. Brian lent him a torch that must have been a real novelty for him because he flashed it – all night – and chopped himself wood to keep the fire going – all night – right outside our van! At 02:30 the jet from London to Johannesburg flew over – the only sign of civilisation for miles.

Ingrid Hardman

Lake Bogoria

Dotted along the lake edge and in the rocks around and above the water are numerous hissing geysers. It looks for all the world as if an over zealous pyromaniac has set off dozens of small fires simultaneously! It was truly an amazing spectacle … an expensive one too.

Ingrid Hardman

at which you will take a right turn onto a potholed tar road, and proceed to the town of Kitale 10 kilometres away.

Diesel was available in Kitale. There is also a supermarket and banking facilities.

Pass through Kitale and proceed north on the A1, a tar road with the odd pothole. After approximately 100 kilometres, take a right turn, onto a good dirt road, to Sigor. From here to Kabernet, via Tot, is roughly 174 kilometres of beautiful bush surrounded by magnificent mountains, waterfalls and sunsets. This is mother nature at her best.

There is no accommodation available along this route, but after a full day's driving, we noticed a church high up on the hills to our right. Taking a chance, we followed the dirt road to the top, and were welcomed by curious locals who were only too happy to let us camp there for the night.

The dirt road eventually connects with the C51, where you will take a left turn and head for the town of Kabernet 30 kilometres away. Do not forget to look back and admire the view.

Diesel was available in Kabernet and fresh vegetables were for sale on the side of the road just as you enter the town.

Continue along the C51 to Marigat. Approximately 40 kilometres later, at a T-junction, you will need to take a right turn onto the B4, which is a good tar road. About 1 kilometre down the B4 take a left turn and proceed for 20 kilometres, along a badly potholed road, to the Loboi Gate at Lake Bogoria.

Lake Bogoria

Although the hot springs and geysers were interesting to see, the entrance fee was exorbitant and it was disappointing to see the local cattle and goats in amongst the zebras. The campsite, called Fig Tree, was situated at the southernmost tip of the lake, nestled in amongst the beautiful fig trees. There were no facilities for campers.

Remember to carry sufficient fresh water for the length of your stay. Entry US$50.00 per person per day, vehicle KSh1 000.00 per day and camping US$15.00 per person per day.

DID YOU KNOW?

Lake Bogoria is a shallow soda lake covering an area of 30 sq kilometres with a maximum depth of nine metres.

Geyser at Lake Bogoria

■ Lake Bogoria to the Masai Mara National Reserve

It is approximately 383 kilometres from Lake Bogoria to the Masai Mara National Reserve.

Proceed back to the entrance gate and make your way to the B4 from there.

Once on the B4, continue south for approximately 113 kilometres to the A104.

The B4 is a tar road with the odd pothole but as you approach the A104 the road will deteriorate even further. Cross over the A104 and head for Narok, via Njoro and Enangiperi, on the C75. This is a good dirt road that could become problematic in the rainy season. If in doubt, ask the local people for advice or take the B3 south of Naivasha.

From Narok, take a left turn onto the B3, which will become the C12, and continue straight on to the Masai Mara National Reserve and the Sekanani Gate.

When passing through Narok, you will cross over a small stream and pass the Kenol fuel station on the left. This is a good spot for refreshments. Diesel cost KSh83.30 per litre.

Masai Mara National Reserve

This is an amazing place that, surprisingly, can be covered in two days.

The first day we explored the eastern end of the park and camped that night outside the Sekanani gate. The second day we explored the western end of the park and camped outside the Talek gate. The following morning we did an early game drive in time to exit the reserve at the Sekanani gate before the 09:00 cut off time.

Armed guards are available, at no cost, to escort you to that point in the Mara River where the wildebeest and zebra cross over from the Serengeti National Park. This is also a safe spot to stop for lunch.

Entry US$80.00 per person per day and KSh1000.00 per vehicle per day.

KENYA – ROUTE PLANNING

THE MAASAI

- The Maasai people originally came from southern Sudan in the Nile Valley.
- The word 'Mara' means spotted or mottled in the Maasai language.
- Maasai homes are called Inkajijik. They are loaf-shaped and made from sticks, grass, mud and cow dung.

- Female lions are never hunted because the Maasai believe that females of every species are the bearers of life.
- Lion hunting is considered a symbolic rite of passage to the Maasai. They consider the experience a personal achievement and a sign of bravery among warriors.

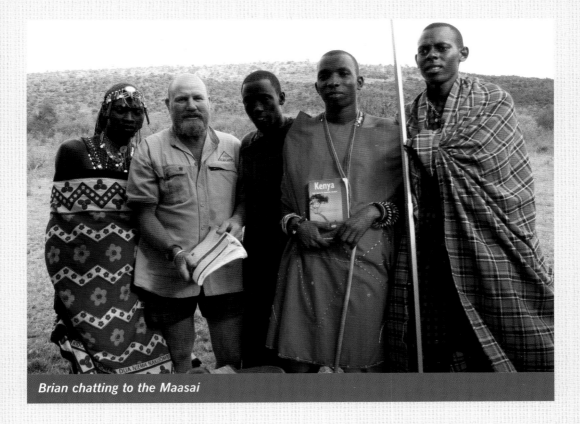
Brian chatting to the Maasai

There are campsites run by the Maasai outside the two main gates. The campsites are well maintained with hot water showers and good security. If you are not sure where to go, proceed to the Masai Mara entrance gate and the Maasai will guide you to a camp for the night.

ROUTE PLANNING – KENYA

DID YOU KNOW:

- The black circular patches on the inner forelegs of zebra are called 'chestnuts,' and are rough pieces of skin that are designed to accommodate the sharp end of the hoof, at rest, when the legs are tucked in.

- The hairs on an elephant's tail are thick and tough and are used as an insect swatter. If the tail is flat against the body, the elephant's mood is generally good.

- Cheetahs are the only cats without retractable claws.

- The mane on the male lion helps to protect the head and neck during vicious encounters with other male lions.

The last mud patch was the longest. There was no way round so we spent the next couple of hours helping everyone out on condition they waited for us to get through. What a job.

KENYA – ROUTE PLANNING

EXCERPT FROM A LETTER SENT HOME

The next morning we were stopped and told by a local gentleman that we would not get through on this road to the Masai Mara. Turning back at this late stage was not an option. Even with chains on the tyres we battled. Mud everywhere.

The last mud patch (**above**) was the longest and it had four vehicles, including a game viewing vehicle carrying tourists, stuck in it. There was no way around so we spent the next couple of hours helping everyone out on condition they waited for us to get through.

What a job. Brian and Neville were covered in mud!

The annual wildebeest migration north, from the Serengeti National Park in Tanzania, to the Masai Mara National Reserve in Kenya.

ROUTE PLANNING – KENYA

I saw the first few plunge in – and then all hell broke loose. It was like the green light going on at the start of the GP – and just as exciting! I got goosebumps watching these animals risking their lives because of an incredible instinct to find grazing. It was one of the most amazing spectacles I've ever seen in Africa. Huge dust clouds from their hooves as they plunged from bank to water, and the sleek wet bodies emerging from the other side and thundering away along the plains is a sight that will stay with me forever.

Ingrid Hardman

■ Masai Mara National Reserve to Olorgasailie Prehistoric Site and Lake Magadi

It is approximately 350 kilometres from the Masai Mara National Reserve to Lake Magadi.

From the Sekanani gate, continue along the C12 to Narok, 94 kilometres away, on a good tar road with the odd pothole. Diesel was available in Narok.

From Narok the C12 becomes the B3, which will eventually connect with the A104. This was a bad section of road under repair.

Once back on the A104, head east to Nairobi. As you enter the city centre, stay on the Uhuru Highway to the traffic circle with Haile Selaisse Road. Take a right turn onto Haile Selaisse Road. From this point on, follow the C58 all the way to Lake Magadi.

Olorgasailie Prehistoric Site

In the 1940s, archaeologists Louis and Mary Leakey discovered stone tools and hand axes **(above)** thought to have been made by *Homo erectus* over half a million years ago. Together with some fossils, these finds have been left in place. A guided tour of the area is available for KSh500.00 per person.

The campsite is situated close by and although very rustic, the view is beautiful, the stars amazing and the peace and quiet will leave you wondering if you're the only person left on the planet.

Camping costs KSh600.00 per person per day.

Lake Magadi

Lake Magadi is the most mineral rich of the soda lakes and is rarely visited by tourists because of its remoteness. The land is barren but beautiful as it blends with the pink, apricot and white colours of the lake. It is surrounded by mountains and although there are no facilities, there are plenty of bush sites from which one can choose to set up camp. If you are a bird-watcher, then this is the place to be.

Lake Magadi

◼ Lake Magadi to Diani Beach

It is approximately 838 kilometres from Lake Magadi to Diani Beach.

Proceed back to Nairobi. Once at the Uhuru Highway/Haile Selaisse Road traffic circle, take a right turn onto the Uhuru Highway, which will become Mombasa Road and then the A109. Proceed to Mombasa 521 kilometres away. This is a notoriously dangerous road on which accidents are common. Watch out for speeding buses and trucks that have no qualms about overtaking on blind corners,

LAKE MAGADI

Lake Magadi is the southernmost Lake in the Kenyan Rift Valley, lying in a catchment of faulted volcanic rocks, north of Tanzania's Lake Natron. Lake Magadi is a saline, alkaline lake, approximately 100 square kilometres in size, that lies in an endorheic basin formed by a graben. The lake is recharged mainly by saline hot springs (temperatures up to 86°C) that discharge into alkaline 'lagoons' around the lake margins. A single species of fish, a cichlid *Alcolapia grahami*, inhabits the hot, highly alkaline waters of this lake basin and is commonly seen in some of the hot spring pools around the shoreline.

a white line or on a rise. They will even flash you to get out of the way!

The initial 50 to 100 kilometres of road is in a poor condition, but it was under repair at the time of our passing.

COLOURFUL TRADE NAMES

- Miracle Hair Salon
- Wonder Price Shop
- Sweatable Fashions
- Nameless Store
- Supernatural Boutique

MAN-EATERS OF TSAVO

Construction of the railway reached the Tsavo River in 1898. During construction of the bridge, lions terrrorised the workers, killing over 130 people before being killed by Colonel Patterson. The lions became known as the 'man-eaters of Tsavo'.

Roughly 26 kilometres past the town of Samburu, take a right turn to Kinango 38 kilometres away. From Kinango, take a left turn to Kwale, and continue straight to the A14 that runs parallel with the sea. Take a right turn onto the A14 and head for Diani Beach a couple of kilometres down the road.

Diani Beach

This area of the coastline is very popular with locals and tourists in peak season. There is lots of accommodation to choose from and the beach is gorgeous. The local people visit the campsites on a regular basis selling fresh fruit, vegetables and fish. There is a bank with an ATM, fuel, restaurants and dhow trips to offshore islands.

Diani Campsite and Cottages

Tel: (040) 3203192
E-mail: dianicampsite@yahoo.com
Web: www.dianicampsite.com.

Situated 2 kilometres from the Diani Nakumatt opposite the Diani Beach Post Office, on the beach side. Camping costs KSh500.00 per person per day.

The Kargs and Days arrived at lunch time with all their news and photographs of the Masai Mara – lion kills, leopard, and getting stuck in the mud! We bought another salmon and more tiger prawns from a vendor for dinner. The stories ended, the fire died down and the moonlight shimmered on the silver sea. A truly magical evening.

Ingrid Hardman

Attractions

Shimba Hills National Reserve

Although we had planned to visit the Shimba Hills National Reserve, approximately 35 kilometres from Diani Beach, the group decided against it. We later learnt from a fellow traveller that the reserve is well worth a visit.

Shimoni

The village of Shimoni sits at the tip of a small peninsula about 67 kilometres south of Diani Beach. There are some interesting ruins, colonial graves and old slave caves. KSh400.00 per person.

■ Diani Beach to Watamu via Kilifi

It is approximately 136 kilometres from Diani Beach to Watamu.

From Diani Beach we made our way north to Mombasa along the A14 to the Likoni Ferry (KSh220.00 per vehicle).

Once back on dry land, continue along Nyerere Road, which will eventually become Digo Road. Digo Road runs for a short distance before veering off to the left and becoming Jomo Kenyatta Road. Continue until you see Ronald Ngala Road on your right. Turn onto Ronald Ngala Road and proceed to Kilifi roughly 55 kilometres to the north on the B8. From Kilifi continue north to Watamu 51 kilometres further on.

Diesel cost KSh85.00 per litre and there are banks with ATM facilities and a supermarket.

Diesel in Watamu cost KSh87.90 per litre. There were no banking facilities.

REMINDER!

If you are the proud owner of timeshare, why not stop over at the Mnarani Club on Malinda Road, Kilifi. Visualise hot showers, a cosy bed, laundry service and restaurant.
A 4x4 traveller's paradise!

The other creatures encountered that night were hundreds of coconut crabs **(left)** – huge things living in snail shells. They were everywhere the fallen coconuts were; their claws and feelers bristling and snapping around our feet. Beryl didn't find it very funny when I picked one up and chased her!

Ingrid Hardman

Mnarani Ruins – Kilifi

Follow the boatyard sign on the left before going over the Kilifi Creek bridge. KSh500.00 per person plus a tip for the guide. The ruins are located on a steep cliff overlooking the Kilifi Creek. Archeological findings suggest that the site was occupied till the late 16th century.

Mnarani Historical Monument

Distant Relatives Ecolodge and Backpackers

Cell: 0770885164
E-mail: distantrelativeskilifi@gmail.com
Web: www.kilifibackpackers.com

Cross over the Kalifi bridge and turn left at the signpost just after Tusky's Supermarket. Proceed down the road for 2.5 kilometres.

Camping costs KSh500.00 per person per day.

Watamu

There is a lot of accommodation to choose from in Watamu, but unfortunately most of it is closed mid-year. Not only is this period out of season but it is also a very windy time of the year when the beautiful beaches are covered in ankle-deep seaweed. We were fortunate enough to be allowed to camp in the grounds of a hotel undergoing renovations.

There is a fishing tackle shop called 'Captain Andy's Fishing Supplies' in the hotel grounds, and for a tiny shop it had a surprising amount of equipment. Some of the lures are called stubby bubbler, wiggle wart, chug bug and hot 'n tot. There was also a sign in the shop that said: 'Always think like a fish no matter how weird it gets!'

Ingrid Hardman

Gede Ruins

Gede Ruins

Web: www.museums.or.ke

This is a very interesting place located about 4 kilometres from Watamu, just off the main Malindi/Mombasa Road, and is one of the principal historical monuments on the coast.

Hidden away in the forest is a vast complex of mosques, palaces and houses made all the more mysterious by the fact that there are no records of its existence in historical texts. It was occupied by at least the 13th century and no one really understands why it was abandoned. KSh600.00 per person and KSh400.00 for the guide.

ROUTE PLANNING – KENYA

Sandgrouse

Approaching Lamu Island

Watamu to Mokowe and Lamu Island

It is approximately 250 kilometres from Watamu to Mokowe.

Make your way back to the B8 and head north to Malindi. From Malindi continue along the B8 to Garsen, roughly 114 kilometres away. Once there, take a left turn onto the C112 to Mokowe. This is a good tar road, with the odd pothole, that will eventually become a dirt road and end at a small harbour. You will be required to leave your vehicle here and take a dhow to Lamu island.

KSh200.00 per night for the car guard and KSh400.00 for the dhow to Lamu island.

The 'car park'. Although dodgy looking, none of the vehicles were interfered with

TIP

Pop in to one of the tiny beachfront shops, buy a piece of material, and have a dress or skirt sewn.

Lamu Island

Lamu Island is very much like Zanzibar only less commercial with few, if any, tourists. On arrival you will be met by many representatives only too willing to help arrange accommodation, fishing trips etc. The longer you stay the cheaper the price.

Subira House

Cell: 0726916686
E-mail: info@subirahouse.com
Web: www.subirahouse.com

Current rates are available on the Subira House website.

■ Mokowe to Garissa

It is approximately 360 kilometres from Mokowe to Garissa.

Proceed back to Garsen and continue north along the B8 to Garissa. The tar road eventually deteriorates and becomes a dirt road, which will slow you down to, at most, 35 kilometres per hour for about 10 kilometres. After this stretch, a good tar road follows. This side of Kenya is hot and dry

LAMU ISLAND (right)

- Arab settlers established a trading post here in the early 16th century.
- Ivory, mangrove poles, tortoiseshell and slaves were exported.
- The population of Lamu is mostly Muslim.
- In 2001, Lamu was added to UNESCO's list of World Heritage Sites.

with no sign of life except for the odd cattle herder. At the T-junction take a right turn to Garissa. There is little of interest in this town but it does have fuel, a Barclays Bank with ATM and a supermarket.

Government Guest House

There are no camping facilities in Garissa, but the manager of the Government Guest House allowed us to camp in the parking area for KSh1 000.00 per person. This includes the use of bathroom facilities in one of the rooms.

Take the first right turn after the bridge over the Tana River. The guest house is situated on the right, just down the road.

■ Garissa to Naro Moru

It is approximately 336 kilometres from Garissa to Naro Moru.

Pass back over the Tana River Bridge and continue straight along the A3, a good tar road followed by potholes and the odd speed hump.

Fuel is readily available the closer you get to Thika. There is a supermarket and banking facilities in Thika but no camping facilities.

SUNDAY, JULY 08, 2007

To describe the road as potholed would be an understatement. Youths on the side of the road armed with spades sporadically toss soil into the craters and then demand payment!

A huge 16-wheeler truck was belly up in the culvert next to the road. Fifty metres down the road was a road sign that said, 'Jesus Saves,' and in small writing below someone had written in black paint, 'No more'!

Our lunch stop was next to a Christian Orthodox Church whose members were in the middle of a service – my word, these people can sing, without musical instruments. Their songs, harmonious and soothingly refreshing in a parched desert land.

The further north we go, the tougher the conditions – there are more flies and heat with fewer provisions, less water, less Internet access and less BEER!

Ingrid Hardman

KENYA – ROUTE PLANNING

MOUNT KENYA

Mount Kenya is 17 057 feet high. It is the highest mountain in Kenya and the second highest in Africa. The several peaks on the mountain were formed by volcanic eruptions. The last eruption was over 2 million years ago. There are several glaciers on Mount Kenya, although they are retreating quickly and no new ice is forming. In less than 30 years the mountain may be completely free of ice. The Gikuyu tribes build their huts with doorways facing the mountain, as they believe it to be God's throne on Earth. The mountain is home to several unique species of animals, including the sykes monkey, cape buffalo and bongo antelope.

The Ol Donyo Sabuk National Park is approximately 60 kilometres before Thika. Camping facilities are available outside the main gate.

From Thika, proceed north on the A2 to Naro Moru along a good tar road. This area is quite built up, so as you approach Naro Moru keep your eyes open for the Naro Moru River Lodge sign.

Naro Moru River Lodge

Cell: 0724082752
E-mail: reservations@naromoruriverlodge.com
Web: www.naromoruriverlodge.com

Situated approximately 1.5 kilometres north of the Naro Moru village, off Nyeri/Nanyuk Road. Activities include bike riding (KSh500.00), nature walks, tennis (KSh250.00), squash (KSh250.00), bird watching and swimming. Safaris to Mt. Kenya can be arranged.

Camping costs KSh1 000.00 per couple with green grass, shade, hot showers and a great view of Mt. Kenya in the early morning.

◼ Naro Moru to Samburu National Reserve

It is approximately 145 kilometres from Naro Moru to the Samburu National Reserve.

From Naro Moru, head north to Nanyuki on the A2. If you didn't restock for the trip north, then Nanyuki is the last stop to do so. There is a supermarket and Barclays Bank and diesel ranges in price from KSh84.99 to KSh86.60 per litre.

Continue along the A2 to Isiolo where diesel will cost KSh88.73 per litre. There is also the 'Da Gunners General Shop' for forgotten bits and pieces.

Approximately 10 kilometres north of Isiolo, the tar road ends and becomes one of Africa's most infamous bad roads! If anything is going to fall apart it will do so on this road!

Forty kilometres from Isiolo, take a left turn after the bridge over the Ewaso Ngiro River. Proceed down the dirt road to the Samburu National Reserve entrance gate.

Samburu National Reserve

The landscape here is a mixture of plains and peaks, scrub desert and savanna. Although only there for a short period of time, we were fortunate enough to see five cheetah, gerenuk, grevy's zebra, vulturine guinea fowl and a million dik-dik!

The campsite was full of backpackers but we managed to find a shady spot under a tree, which a lone male elephant proceeded to knock around during the night in pursuit of his favourite food!

Entry US$70.00 per person per day and KSh1 000.00 per day for the vehicle.

Should you not wish to visit the reserve, there is a community camp situated along the dirt road leading to the reserve, based on the riverbank, and a short distance from the Samburu entrance gate. Camping costs US$15.00 per person per day.

■ Samburu National Reserve to Wamba

It is approximately 55 kilometres from Samburu National Reserve to Wamba.

Exit the Samburu National Reserve at the west gate and follow the dirt road to Wamba 55 kilometres to the north. The dirt road is a combination of stone and sand with powder dust, ruts and dry riverbed crossings, but the beautiful scenery makes up for any inconvenience. After 40 kilometres take a left turn and head for Wamba 15 kilometres away.

Wamba

Wamba is a small town in the middle of nowhere with little to offer the few visitors that do pass through. We were fortunate enough to be offered a spot to camp in the church grounds and spent the afternoon listening to the most beautiful choir I have

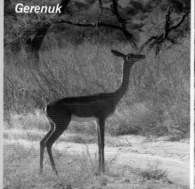

Gerenuk

Grevy's Zebra

Reticulated Giraffe

ever heard. With goose bumps, I managed to record several minutes and will treasure this small moment for years to come.

Wamba to Lake Turkana

It is approximately 342 kilometres from Wamba to Lake Turkana

Follow the C78 northwest to Maralal, approximately 110 kilometres away, on a fairly good dirt road. Pass through Maralal and head north on the C77 towards South Horr. The dirt road is in good condition but some sections pass over bed rock, which is uneven and slow going with an average speed of 37 kilometres per hour, but with scenery so breathtaking you won't want to go any faster! Unable to reach South Horr before nightfall, we camped in a dry riverbed with two armed Samburu men to watch over us!

Twenty-five kilometres north of South Horr there is a Y-junction at which you will need to take a left turn. Lake Turkana is approximately 50 kilometres north of this point.

Maralal is the last stop for supplies before heading north. Fuel and banking facilities were available but please note that there is no ATM.

Northern Kenya

Lake Turkana – The Jade Sea

Lake Turkana is an amazing place that should be on everyone's itinerary when visiting Kenya. But be warned: it's not for the faint hearted!

The wind blows all day and all night, 365 days of the year, making daily chores and sleeping in a rooftop tent a challenge of note. Even the rubber duck battled to stay upright on the water!

However, the beauty of the harsh landscape with its extinct volcanoes surrounded by the green waters of the lake and its abundance of large Nile Perch, made it all worth while. Finding the right campsite would have been the cherry on top!

Look out for a small clump of thorn trees **(top right)** as you approach the lake. At this point the dirt road swings to the right and on to Loyangalani. As you start to descend towards the thorn trees, keep an eye open for a dirt track leading off to the left. Follow this for approximately 25 kilometres where you will find a basic campsite well sheltered from the wind. There are other potential sites en route should you not wish to travel so far off the beaten track.

At times the road was thick sand, but before long it became rocky, not unlike the Richtersveld.

The valley changed to a flat, grey moonscape dotted with rock piles like gigantic cairns. Then, finally, miles and miles of black volcanic rocks and stones – smoothed by eons of wind, water and sand … as if a hailstorm of immeasurable proportions had rained upon the stark valley. It was literally a desert of rocks.

Lake Turkana glimmered in the distance, its startling turquoise a complete contrast to the seared landscape. Hours of grinding through rocks followed until we reached the lakeshore. Finding a spot sheltered from the ceaseless wind was impossible.

Ingrid Hardman

KENYA – ROUTE PLANNING

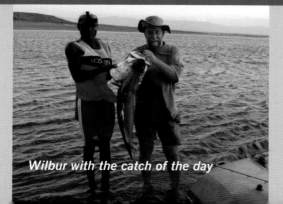

Wilbur with the catch of the day

EXCERPT FROM A LETTER SENT HOME

The wind never stops blowing and is stronger at night. We battled to find a spot out of the wind and had to use two pegs to hold each awning leg down. Dust everywhere. I slept in the truck one night and outside the next. No sleep. Lovely big fish though – 20 to 25 kilograms.

We ate well!

Lake Turkana

All visitors to this remote area of Kenya should be self-sufficient. The ability to sleep in the back of your vehicle, as opposed to on top, would be an added bonus!

◼ Lake Turkana to Loyangalani

It is approximately 35 kilometres from Lake Turkana to Loyangalani.

Proceed back to the main dirt road and continue north towards Loyangalani.

Palm Shade Camp

Cell: 0726714768

The campsite is small but nicely situated under the shade of palm trees. We opted for one of the stick and doum-palm dwellings (KSh1 200.00), which despite their haphazard construction, proved to be remarkably spacious and cool. Camping costs KSh700.00 per couple.

The town of Loyangalani has little to offer passing tourists, but for KSh300.00 per person, a community walk to meet the Turkana tribes people can be arranged.

The huts around here are made of a framework of sticks that are covered with cow or camel hide and shaped like giant burger buns! The men were out fishing and herding their animals. The women were dressed in dull brown cottons – many of them of animal hide with neck beads and earrings still the order of the day. The graveyard consists of piles of stones above unmarked graves. In past times, bodies were wrapped in animal skins and left under a tree for the hyenas. In this way, it was believed that the person's spirit would live on in the animal.

KENYA – ROUTE PLANNING

Turkana Tribe and traditional dwelling

Loyangalani to Marsabit

It is approximately 260 kilometres from Loyangalani to Marsabit.

The road northeast from Loyangalani to North Horr, and eventually Marsabit, involves crossing the Chalbi Desert. The trip took us ten hours to complete, driving over salt pans, through powder dust and over stones and ruts. It's a long day in a harsh environment with high temperatures, no water and only the odd camel for comfort. Make sure you are well prepared for any eventuality before attempting this road.

There is a fuel station, bank and hospital in Marsabit. However, the fuel supply in Moyale is irregular, but there is fuel in Ethiopia.

Lake Turkana

- Don't assume tyre tracks will lead you in the right direction.
- Carry plenty of water.
- Warning – deep ruts may be encountered when crossing on and off a bridge.

Marsabit National Park

Proceed into Marsabit and turn left at the Shell garage. Continue on to the traffic circle and turn right. Follow the signboards from here. The campsite is grassed and offers some shade, a long drop toilet and cold water shower. The entry fee is US$25.00 per person for a 24-hour period, KSh35 000.00 for the vehicle and US$30.00 per person to camp. Not cheap for a night in the bush with a cold water shower! On arrival, check that the water supply to the campsite has been turned on!

■ Marsabit National Park to the Moyale Border Post and Ethiopia

It is approximately 256 kilometres from Marsabit National Park to Moyale.

Proceed north along the A2 to the border town of Moyale. This is without a doubt the worst road we have encountered on the trip – three hours to do 100 kilometres. Fortunately, it is now tarred!

Chalbi Desert

Scrubby bushes, scraggly trees, sandstorms, rocks and no shortage of dust – plumes of it, actually – billowing up and around the truck. We were at the back today so we had the full dose! Part of the route was an enormous saltpan **(above)** – it looked as if we were going through snow – and then again more desert, complete with camels and mirages. No real roads, but tracks all over the place.

Ingrid Hardman

The Great North Road!

ROUTE PLANNING – KENYA

The road is badly corrugated, rocky and passes through the uninviting Dida Galgalu desert. Brian got a puncture and we rattled and squeaked worse than ever before. All the vehicles are taking a battering – I wince every time we hit a rock. We had to stop several times to solder Dave's radiator and then his bush rubbers came off and he lost the spacers. We had been warned at police roadblocks that it is not advisable to stop along this road, but we had no option. The 'great north road' is NOT great! At the border we noticed that our main diesel tank had sprung a leak … something else to sort out!

Ingrid Hardman

ETHIOPIA

N

0   100 km

Map Labels

ERITREA

Aksum · 1 · Adigrat
3
Simien Mtns. National Park

Debark · Mekelle
1

Gondar · Maychew

Lake Tana

Lalibela
Woldiya

DJIBOUTI

SUDAN

3

1

Debre Markos ·

Fiche

SOMALIA

3 · 1 · Debre Berhan

Addis Ababa
4 · Mojo

6

Shashemene · Dinsho

Sodo · Wondo Genet

Bale Mountains National Park and the Harenna Forest

Nechisar National Park
Arba Minch

Omo Valley · Konso

Yabelo

SOMALIA

6

Moyale

KENYA

Moyale Border Post

🏛 **World Heritage Sites**

ETHIOPIA – ROUTE PLANNING

The national flag symbolises the honor and beauty of the Ethiopian nation. Green represents the fertility of the country, yellow the religious freedom found there, and red the lives sacrificed in the protection of national integrity. Recently, the Council of Peoples' Representatives endorsed the proclamation of a new emblem on the national flag. The new emblem will have a radiant star with equidistant rays to show the equality of all ethnic groups as well as creed and gender equity. The shining rays from the star testify to a bright future for Ethiopia, and surrounding the emblem will be a blue background to denote peace and democracy in Ethiopia.

■ Ethiopia at a Glance

- Highlights included the Omo Valley, Wondo Genet, Bale Mountains National Park, Lalibela, Aksum and Gondar.

- Drive on the right-hand side of the road.

- Diesel is cheap but not always readily available in outlying areas. Stick to the rules of the road and fill up every time you pass a fuel station.

- The roads were in good condition but watch out for rocks and spontaneous waterfalls if caught in a rain storm.

- There are few road signs in Ethiopia. Although I have provided directions, they should always be verified, where possible, to avoid delay and diesel wastage. Most of the main roads are designated a number for identification. For example, the main road north from Moyale to Mojo is Route 6 and from Mojo to Addis Ababa is Route 4.

- Bus and truck drivers are a danger to fellow road users.

- The children will constantly pester you for Birr1.00.

- Petty crime does exist so do not leave anything of value lying around.

- The local people are very helpful and will demand payment for their services, even if all they did was pass you the spanner!

- Fruit and vegetables are not as freely available en route, but each village does have a market day once a week.

- Accommodation rates are good but the level of maintenance/hygiene could be better.

- Most basic amenities we are familiar with back home are available in Ethiopian shops. However, the hard-boiled sweets were not great and in some cases the biscuits were soft.

- Before taking a photograph of an individual, a price must be negotiated and agreed upon. Photographs of a crowd do not generally require payment. Make sure you have lots of Birr1.00's.

- All buses have blaring music emanating from loudspeakers mounted on the roof.

- It is expensive to view Ethiopia's churches and other sites of historical interest.

ROUTE PLANNING – ETHIOPIA

DID YOU KNOW?

- Dula – A wooden staff used by Ethiopian highlanders when travelling
- Falasha – Ethiopian Jew
- Tej – Wine made from honey
- Faranji – Foreigner
- Gari – Horse-drawn cart

■ General Information

Airlines

South African Airways
506 Bole Road, Addis Ababa
Tel: (011) 5537880
Cell: 0911510961

British Airways
Hilton Hotel, Menelik 11 Ave, Addis Ababa
Tel: (011) 5170000

Bole International Airport
Tel: (011) 6650499

ETHIOPIA – ROUTE PLANNING

ETHIOPIAN FOLK TALE

Once upon a time there was a donkey, a dog and a goat who wanted to go on a journey together. They hired a taxi and off they went. After a while, the donkey paid his fare and got out. The dog also paid, never received his change, and got out. The goat got out too, but never paid. To this day, and whenever a vehicle passes, the donkey plods on, the dog chases its change and the goat scatters!

Border Crossing

The Ethiopian border post at Moyale opens at 08:00.

A single entry visa, valid for one month, costs US$50.00. A three-month visa costs US$ 75.00.

Visas are valid from the date of arrival, not the day of issue.
Web: www.ethiopia.org

Church Etiquette

Remove your shoes before entering.

Wear clothing that covers all parts of the body.

Avoid smoking, eating and drinking.

Do not use a flash when taking photographs of paintings.

Make a donation after your visit.

Climate

The Omo Valley region to the south west is hot and dry with an average daytime temperature of 34°C. The rainy season falls between April and September. Dirt roads may become impassable during this time.

The highlands to the north are cooler with an average daytime temperature of 30°C. Night-time temperatures can be as low as 15°C. The rainy season falls between August and September. Visiting the Simien Mountains is not recommended during this time as paths are slippery and the magnificent views are hidden by low cloud cover.

To the east, snow falls on the Bale Mountains mid-year, and temperatures can fall as low as -2°C.

Diplomatic Missions

South Africa
Nifasilk Lafto, Kabele 03, Addis Ababa
Tel: (011) 3711002/1017
E-mail: dha@ethionet.et

Egypt
Sidist Kilo, Gule, Kabele 02, Addis Ababa
Tel: (011) 1226422
E-mail: embassy.addisababa@mfa.gov.eg

Sudan
Kirkoss KK, Kabele 10, Addis Ababa
Tel: (011) 5516477
E-mail: sudan.embassy@telecom.net.et

Dress Etiquette

Ethiopians are conservative in their dress. Visitors should respect their way of life and dress accordingly.

Electricity

The electricity supply is 220V with a variety of sockets.

Power cuts occur during the rainy season and power surges are common.

Medical

Compulsory vaccinations: Yellow Fever.
Recommended vaccinations: Hepatitis A & B, Meningitis, Polio, Rabies, Typhoid.
Precautions: Malaria risk.

Bethel General Hospital – Addis Ababa
Tel: (011) 3495475/76

Money

The unit of currency is the Birr.

ATMs are only available in the larger towns and cities.

Public Holidays

Ethiopian Christmas	– January 07
Epiphany (Timkat)	– January 19
Adwa Victory Day	– March 02
Easter	– Variable
Labour Day	– May 01
Freedom Day	– May 05
Downfall of the Dergue	– May 28
Ethiopian New Year	– September 11

Rules of the Road and Vehicle Requirements

Drive on the right-hand side of the road.

Visitors may drive for up to three months on a valid driving license that has been issued in their country of residence.

The wearing of seatbelts is mandatory.

The recommended speed limit is 30–50 kilometres per hour in towns and villages and 100 kilometres per hour on all other roads. This may vary as per the regulatory traffic signs.

ZA sticker is required.

Cellphone usage is prohibited whilst driving.

ETHIOPIA – ROUTE PLANNING

As we began the trek eastwards through villages of wooden huts, all neatly fenced off with cactus plants, a patchwork of farmland lush from all the rain melted into equally lush hills and valleys. These hills and valleys were threaded with streams and clumps of gnarled trees, with lavender, wildflowers and swathes of red-hot pokers decorating the gullies and roadside.

Ingrid Hardman

Proceed with caution if travelling at night. Most local vehicles have inadequate lighting, park irresponsibly and – believe it or not – there are numerous hyenas out and about.

Landmines remain a problem in the northernmost regions of Ethiopia along the border with Eritrea.

Watch out for pedestrians.

A first aid kit is compulsory.

Service Telephone Numbers and Area Codes

International Code for Ethiopia: +251

Area Codes: Addis Ababa 011, Aksum 034, Arba Minch 046, Gondar 058, Lalibela 033

Emergency – Tel: 991/997

Taxis

Blue and white coloured taxis are usually available at main traffic intersections and outside hotels and restaurants. It is important to negotiate the fare prior to departure. The drivers are very courteous and extremely helpful with an extensive knowledge of the city. For the duration of our stay in Addis Ababa, we negotiated a daily rate with one specific driver, who spent his day driving us around to spares shops, supermarkets and areas of interest within the city.

Vehicle Assistance

Ethio Lakes
BMW, Land Rover and Ford specialist garage
Tel: (011) 431492/93
Web: www.ethiolakes.com

Moenco
Official Toyota Dealer
Tel: (011) 6613688
Web: www.moencoethiopia.com

Websites and Books for Additional Information

Web: www.wikitravel.org
www.ethiovisit.com
www.sacred-destinations.com
www.sacredsites.com

'The Sign and the Seal' by Graham Hancock

'Notes from the Hyena's Belly' by Nega Mezlekia

'Birds of Ethiopia and Eritrea' by John Ash and John Atkins

ROUTE PLANNING – ETHIOPIA

Ethiopian coins were amongst the earliest coins of any country to carry a Christian symbol i.e. the cross. These coins were found by shepherds near Aksum.

ETHIOPIAN SAINTS

Most churches we visited in Ethiopia were adorned with beautiful paintings of what appear to be mythical creatures, but without a prior knowledge of what it all means, one is left a little baffled and unable to fully appreciate their beauty.

Clockwise from left:
Abuna Aregawi, St. Gebre Manfus Kiddus, St. Tekla Haimanot and Abuna Samuel

Abuna Aregawi

While wandering at the foot of a cliff, Abuna Aregawi spotted a large plateau high above him. Deciding it was a good spot for a quiet hermit's life, he prayed to God for assistance. Immediately a large python stretched down and lifted him onto the plateau.

Abuna Samuel

Accompanied by a devoted lion, this saint preached and performed many miracles, and is usually seen in paintings with the lion beside him.

St. Eostateos

This saint is said to have arrived in Ethiopia, along the Nile from Egypt, on three large stones. Thereafter water continued to obey him, and whenever he chose to cross a river or lake, the waters parted before him.

St. Gabriel

God's messenger is usually depicted cooling the flames of a fire containing three youths condemned by Nebuchadnezzar – Meshach, Shadrach and Abednego.

St. Gebre Manfus Kiddus

While preaching peace to the wild animals in the desert, this Ethiopian Francis of Assisi came across a bird dying of thirst. Lifting the bird up, he allowed it to drink the water from his eye. He is usually depicted clad in furs with leopards and lions at his feet. The little bird hovers above him.

St. George

Regarded as the patron saint of Ethiopia, St. George is featured in most churches. He is portrayed on a white horse as the great dragon slayer, and the damsel in distress is a girl called Brutawit from Beirut.

St. Tekla Haimanot

This saint prayed for seven years, standing on one leg, until the other finally withered and fell off. During this time the only sustenance he received was one seed a year from a bird. For his devotion, God awarded him three sets of wings. He is normally depicted in his bishop's attire with the detached leg flying off to heaven.

A TRADITIONAL ETHIOPIAN TALE

Once upon a time, in a land far away, the donkeys were tired of their role as beasts of burden. So they called a meeting and decided to send a representative to God to plead their cause and end their suffering at the hands of man.

Many years have passed since then, and their representative has not yet returned, but the donkeys wait patiently, ever hopeful. Every time they meet one another, they put their heads together and ask, 'Has our envoy returned yet?'

All living creatures yearn for their freedom.

■ Moyale Border Post to Moyale

Moyale

A clean quiet town and a good spot to stop for a couple of days to carry out any necessary repairs. Fuel is cheaper here than in Kenya but the supply tends to be erratic.

Bekele Molla Hotel

Tel: (046) 4410030
Cell: 0115514601
E-mail: langano@bekelemollahotels.com
Web: bekelemollahotels.com

Birr480.00 per day for a double bed and cold water shower. Good security and ample space to carry out vehicle repairs. Although the place could have done with a good maintenance and cleaning plan, it was ideal for our needs and by this stage of the trip we weren't too perturbed!

Kockot Hotel

Situated down the road from the Bekele Molla Hotel and easily identified by its bright yellow signboard. It is here that we first experienced Ethiopian cuisine.

Injera with a spicy stew

ETHIOPIA – ROUTE PLANNING

INJERA

Injera is the staple source of carbohydrates in Ethiopia. It looks like a large pancake with a foam rubber texture and is made from tef (a grain unique to Ethiopia). Although of little nutritional value, it's served with a meal and used to scoop food into your mouth.

> The first camel in the train holds everyone up, but it is the last which gets the beating.
> *Ethiopian Proverb*

Moyale to the Omo Valley

Due to an increase in hostile activities in northern Kenya, southern Sudan and northern Uganda, it was recommended that travellers not venture into the Omo Valley. However, a local guide by the name of Biruk Desalegn assured us that we would be perfectly safe and agreed to take us into the Omo Valley for a period of five days. With Biruk's extensive knowledge on the different tribes, their cultural heritage and different languages, the decision to visit the Omo Valley turned out to be one of the highlights of our trip.

We passed through some interesting places with names like Weyto, Omorate, Key Afar and Jinka. At each one we met different tribespeople, all dressed in their traditional clothing with an assortment of body art.

We also visited a couple of villages and marvelled at their way of life, viewed 'New York' and passed through some magnificent scenery. The dirt roads were in good condition, fuel was available in Yabelo and Konso and accommodation was in either a local hotel or basic campsite. This is a part of Africa every traveller should see, before its people and their culture are lost forever.

Biruk Desalegn lives near the Moyale border post in Ethiopia. He is well known in the area so just ask around and the local people will be able to guide you to his home/office.

Make sure all details of the 'tour' and payment required are on paper (and signed) to avoid complications at the end of the day.

WEDNESDAY, JULY 18, 2007

Another interesting discovery is their calendar. Today is July 11, 1999 and they will celebrate the new millennium on September 11! Already T-shirts are on sale with '2000 – new millennium' printed on them. Even their time is different by several hours. Their day begins at 6:00 and not at midnight like ours – a real bummer when you're booking flights etc! They have 13 months in a year, each with 30 days, except the 13th month, which only has five days!

Ingrid Hardman

You could order rice, vegetables and goat (stewed, grilled, spicy and hot) – rather like those thin lamb ribs I buy for the braai at home. Actually, the food was great and the girls shared a bottle of local red wine. Farouk changed our US$ for Birr, taught us to clap loudly twice for a waiter, and joined us for dinner. It is very safe to walk around at night. There is almost no crime and the banks have no security guards!

Ingrid Hardman

In the Bena tribe **(right)**, for example, the men shave half their heads, giving them a Mohawk/Native American look – very regal! They have beads on their arms and legs, and some paint their legs with white and blue paint.

The women have shortish braided hair and wear skirts of cowhide. They are either bare breasted or wear cow hide tank tops. The older women have wide neckbands, embedded with cowrie shells and beads.

The rocky campsite in Jinka is set above a noisy main road on which buses trundle back and forth with loudspeakers mounted on their roofs, blaring forth the local music. We left our vehicles at the camp and decided to catch the local 'taxi' instead. The taxi was in fact a three-wheeler tuc-tuc. There were seven of us, and a conductor hanging off the back to stop any 'hangers-on' and to collect the fare.

The main reason for going to the market was to see the Mursi tribe **(below right)**. Mursi women, at the age of 18 or so, have their four lower front teeth removed and a slit made between the lower lip and the gum. A clay plate is inserted and as the hole gets bigger, the plate size increases. Sometimes they leave the plates out and the stretched skin hangs around their chin. Mursi men have stick fights and the victor is carried off by a group of women who decide which of them will marry him! Oh, well … different strokes …

Ingrid Hardman

JINKA MARKET DAY

- Onions
- Tomatoes
- Pineapple
- Ginger
- Beans
- Pawpaw
- Bananas
- Butter
- Honey
- Beads

■ Omo Valley to the Nechisar National Park

It is approximately 95 kilometres from Konso to Arba Minch.

Having made our way back to Konso and bid farewell to Biruk, we made our way north to Arba Minch, approximately 95 kilometres away along a good dirt road. Arba Minch is the largest town in southern Ethiopia and is divided into two parts. Arba Minch Shecha is set on an escarpment overlooking Lake Abaya to the north and Lake Chamo to the south. Four kilometres down the escarpment is Arba Minch Sikela.

Fuel, banking facilities and supermarkets are available.

Mora Heights Hotel

Cell: 0911727395
E-mail: selam@moraheightshotel.com
Web: www.moraheightshotel.com

Situated in Arba Minch, 15 minutes from the local airport.

Single room: US$50.60
Double room: US$75.60
Breakfast is included.

Nechisar National Park

Cell: 0468840408/09
Web: www.nechisarnationalpark.com

When I first read about the Nechisar National Park, the travel books painted a beautiful picture. It wasn't until we arrived at the park that it all became clear – there were no animals! In a 24-hour period we saw a lion, a zebra, a couple of dik dik and a troop of baboons. The designated campsite was awful and the night was devoid of all the usual animal sounds. It was only later that we learnt the park had been 'cleaned out' by poachers. However, the scenery was beautiful and we managed to find a pretty spot to camp down by the lake.

Continue through the town to the second traffic circle and turn right. This will take you down the escarpment to Arba Minch Sikela.

ETHIOPIA – ROUTE PLANNING

DID YOU KNOW?

- The name Nechisar means 'white grass' in Amharic.

- The peculiar dark red colour of Lake Abaya is caused by suspended hydroxide in its waters.

- The ridge of land that divides Lake Abaya and Lake Chamo is known as the 'Bridge of God' or 'Heaven' for the beautiful views from it.

As you approach Arba Minch Sikela, look out for the National Park's booking office, situated on the left-hand side of the road, before the church and up from the old Mobile fuel station.

Birr90.00 per person entry fee, Birr20.00 for the vehicle and Birr40.00 per person to camp. The fee charged is for a 24-hour period.

From the booking office, continue straight into town to the traffic circle, that has a statue of a man with a lion. Take a right turn and proceed for about one kilometre. Turn right onto a dirt road, which will lead you to the entrance gate.

Attractions in the Area

Dorze and Chencha

Situated in the Guge Mountains, approximately 36 kilometres north of Arba Minch Shecha, the Dorze people are well known for their beehive huts **(right)** and are skilled farmers, knowledgeable in the prevention of soil erosion. The town of Chencha is best known for its beautiful woven cotton **(top right)**. Try and plan your visit to coincide with their colourful market day for a more enjoyable experience.

The huts made by the Dorze people stand approximately 12 metres high and look like a giant beehive. Made with hardwood poles, bamboo and thatched with enset leaves, these huts can survive for up to 60 years! Most are surrounded by a small garden with an assortment of vegetables, spices and tobacco.

From Arba Minch Sikela, take a right turn at the traffic circle with the statue. Cross the bridge and take a left turn, heading towards the mountains. Watch out for people, cows, baboons, goats, vendors and the odd pothole! After the second bridge you will find the turn-off to Chencha.

■ Arba Minch to Wondo Genet

It is approximately 282 kilometres from Arba Minch to the Wondo Genet Resort Hotel.

Follow the above directions back to the Chencha turn-off.

Continue past the turn-off, and head in a northerly direction to the town of Sodo – on a gravel road with an average speed of 45 kilometres per hour in certain sections.

Once you reach Sodo, proceed up the main road towards the communication tower. At the Y-junction, take a right turn onto a tar road – with the occasional pothole.

Fuel was available in Sodo.

Ploughing the fields, as in most parts of rural Africa, is done using oxen power, and cotton weaving, using looms and bobbins the old medieval way, is still the main occupation here. Colourful scarves, cloths and 'shammas' are sold on the side of the road.

Old women carry enormous stacks of grass and wood on their backs, bent almost double by years of hard labour.

The market here was completely different to any other encountered. Communal tobacco is smoked through a long bamboo and they all line up with their cups for a scoop of local brew made from sorghum.

Driving back to Arba Minch, we found a disused Mobil garage with a ramp, and decided to do an oil change. Wilbur donned his gumboots and went under the van, promptly stepping into a hole of oil that flooded into his boots!

Ingrid Hardman

Road sign highlighting the dangers of irresponsible sex and AIDS.

Continue on to Shashemene approximately 134 kilometres away. As you enter the town, take a right turn at the T-junction. Continue for one kilometre then take a left turn, followed by a right turn onto a rutted dirt road. Fourteen kilometres further on, take a left turn and proceed to the Wondo Genet Resort Hotel.

Diesel was available in Shashemene for Birr15.48 per litre. Banking facilities were also available and an assortment of fruit and vegetables can be purchased form the local people along the dirt road leading to the hotel.

Wondo Genet Resort Hotel

This 1970-styled hotel is a stone's throw away from the hot springs. Although there is no designated area for campers, the spot allocated for our use was no worse than some of the campsites we had already stayed in. Besides, the hot springs made it all worthwhile.

The forgotton, Lalibela

Hot Springs

Situated about 300 metres from the Wondo Genet Resort Hotel, with free entry for hotel guests. The gates open around 06:00 and close at 22:00. Admission costs Birr 25.00 per person. All visitors must shower before entering the pools. This is a recommended stop for all 4x4 travellers with body aches and pains. Not only will you feel better, you will also be a darn site cleaner!

The main pool is emptied and cleaned on a Wednesday. Obviously the weekends are a lot busier, so plan your visit to fit in-between.

WONDO GENET

- The name Wondo Genet means 'place in heaven' in Amharic.
- Guided walks into the surrounding hills is a must for bird watchers. Look out for the endemic yellow-fronted parrot, the black-headed forest oriole and the golden-backed woodpecker.

■ Wondo Genet to the Bale Mountains National Park

It is approximately 185 kilometres from Wondo Genet to the Bale Mountains.

Follow the dirt road from the Wondo Genet Resort Hotel back to the T-junction. Take a right turn and continue for approximately 14 kilometres. Take a left turn followed by a right and you are back at Sheshamene. Pass through the town back to the T-junction and take a right turn. After approximately 6 kilometres take a left turn to Gobe and the Bale Mountains National Park, 158 kilometres to the east. This section of the road is dirt with the odd pothole.

Approximately 185 kilometres from Wondo Genet, just outside the village of Dinsho, look out for a signboard on the right advertising Dinsho Lodge. Take a right turn and follow the dirt road to the 'lodge/ headquarters' of the Bale Mountains National Park.

Words cannot describe the stark beauty of Bale. The road ascends into the mist-covered rocky highlands, past trickling streams of crystal water. Small white bushes, and lobelia plants that look like giant candles in candlesticks, lie scattered across the landscape with ice rats scampering into their holes as we approach. The small streams become lakes, hosting blue winged geese, plovers and ducks, and finally we were rewarded with our first sighting of the rare Ethiopian wolf.

By morning, the mist had cleared but it was still cloudy and very cold at 2°C! Yesterday's mist obscured the prolific birdlife (some endemic to Ethiopia), and plants hugging the marshy ground. Delicate wild flowers in pinks, blues and whites, nestled in the spongy hollows. It was so exquisite!

Ingrid Hardman

ETHIOPIA – ROUTE PLANNING

We drove through forests of gnarled misshapen trees covered in moss and lichen, with 'old man's beard' hanging from the branches, above a carpet of ferns and moss on the forest floor. It was like something straight out of a Grimm Brothers' fairy tale. It was incredibly beautiful.

Dinsho Lodge

It was freezing cold when we arrived at Dinsho Lodge (July/August) and the high rainfall made it impossible to find a suitable campsite. Forced to camp in the parking lot, we soon discovered that Dinsho Lodge was nothing but a disused building in a bad state of disrepair. With only one toilet and cold running water, no one 'bathed' that night! We managed to get a fire going in what was once the lounge area and sat huddled together until the wood ran out! Brian and I found a pile of blankets in one of the rooms and decided we would be a lot warmer under them than in the rooftop tent!

Bale Mountains National Park

E-mail: info@balemountains.org
Web: www.balemountains.org

The entry fee is Birr150.00 per couple per day,
Birr20.00 per vehicle per day,
Birr60.00 per day for the guide and
Birr40.00 per day to camp.

Although there are designated campsites within the park, the facilities are poor to non-existent. At 4 300 metres it was very cold but the beauty of the park made it all worthwhile.

Lobelia plant

Wild flowers

ROUTE PLANNING – ETHIOPIA

Brian radioed to say he had no brakes. The pins had jumped out and he had lost the brake shoes – the second time he has had this problem. Luckily he had spare shoes and a tent peg was cut up for the pins! Bush mechanics! I remarked on a strange chemical smell and, to cut a long story short, the battery under the seat was arching, cooking, actually! Another thing we have to sort out in Addis Ababa.

Ingrid Hardman

The Ethiopian wolf

Harenna Forest

The Harenna Forest lies within the boundaries of the Bale Mountains National Park and is situated at the base of the Harenna Escarpment, which splits the park in two. The drive down is very scenic and the campsite, although basic, was very pretty. A guided walk through the forest will bring back memories of childhood stories on fairies, witches and gnomes.

ETHIOPIA – ROUTE PLANNING

DID YOU KNOW?

Thirty-two percent of frog species are endemic to Ethiopia. Biologists recently discovered four new species in the Harenna Forest, and have observed some peculiar adaptations to their environment. For example, one appears to have lost his ears and another has forgotten how to hop!

■ Bale Mountains National Park to Ziway

It is approximately 280 kilometres from Dinsho Lodge to Ziway.

Retrace your steps back to Shashemene. Approximately 162 kilometres from Dinsho Lodge, as you approach Shashemene, take a left turn at the T-junction, followed by a right turn onto the main road (Route 6) north to Ziway and Addis Ababa.

Ziway

There is not much of interest in Ziway, but we did manage to see some beautiful water birds on the lake. Fuel was available at Birr19.65 per litre.

Bekele Molla Hotel

Tel: (046) 4412571
E:mail: langano@bekelemollahotels.com
Web: www.bekelemollahotels.com

Situated adjacent to the Shell garage on entering Ziway. A double room costs Birr524.00.

We left Ziway for Addis Ababa – just another sprawling city. Actually, it is the third highest capital city in the world. It was pretty shattering to encounter intersections with up to eight roads all converging into an enormous central point – minus the traffic circle! Bear in mind that we are driving on the wrong side of the road here! We just took our cue from the other drivers and did what they did. A few times we made a wrong move and had some angry gestures and hooting directed at us. It's just as confusing when you are on foot. We are so programmed to look another way for traffic, and now it's whizzing by from the wrong direction – I almost got whacked several times!

Ingrid Hardman

It was quite late when we pulled into the Bekele Molla Hotel. We have stayed with them before, but this time our room had a hot shower, and a loo with a seat. All for only Birr524.00 – what luxury!

Ingrid Hardman

■ Ziway to Addis Ababa

It is approximately 170 kilometres from Ziway to Addis Ababa.

Continue north, along the main road (Route 6), to Mojo approximately 96 kilometres away. This is a good tar road with the odd pothole. Watch out for animals.

At Mojo, N8°35.252' E39°07.470', you will need to take a left turn to Debre Zeyit (Route 4) and head for Addis Ababa, roughly 66 kilometres away.

Our arrival in Addis Ababa was scary! We had no idea where to go and even if we did, it would have been a battle to get there! If you find yourself in a similar predicament, pull over and negotiate a price with a local taxi driver, identified by their blue and white coloured vehicles, to get you where you need to be.

Route 4 will bring you into Addis Ababa on the Debre Zeyit Road, which will eventually become Beyene Aba Sebsib Avenue. This avenue will lead you to Meskel Square where you will need to take a right turn onto Jomo Kenyatta Avenue. This avenue will eventually become Haile Gebreselassie Road and it is along this section of road that you will find the Debre Damo Hotel and the Axum Hotel next door to it. To get to Lalibela, you will need to continue out of the city along the Haile Gebreselassie Road.

Debre Damo Hotel

Tel: (011) 6612630
E-mail: reservation@debredamohotel.com
Web: www. debredamohotel.com

Under renovation at the time of our stay, this hotel looks better on the inside than it does on the outside. There is a large central courtyard with ample parking and good security. A single room cost US$72.00, standard room US$88.00 and twin room US$116.00. Breakfast is included.

As a result of the renovations, there was no extra space to carry out vehicle repairs. Management at the Axum Hotel agreed to let us use their service bay, so we moved next door!

ETHIOPIA – ROUTE PLANNING

ATTRACTIONS IN ADDIS ABABA

- **Ethiopian National Museum** – with the Ethiopian civilisation being one of the oldest in the world, the artifacts within the museum span thousands of years.
- **Red Terror Museum** – learn about the horrors of the derg that led to the well known famine of the 1990's. Most of the employees are survivors and will tell you stories of their experiences.
- **St. George's Cathedral** – built in 1896 to commemorate Ethiopia's victory over the Italians. The interior is beautifully decorated with huge paintings and mosaics.

Alex

ANGEL IN DISGUISE

We negotiated a price with a local taxi driver, named Alex, to be our chauffeur for the duration of our stay in Addis Ababa. It was by far the easiest way to get around. His knowledge of the city made it a pleasure to shop for spares, sort out visas from the various embassies, buy groceries and view the city sights. Thank you, Alex.

Axum Hotel

Tel: (011) 6613916
E-mail: axum.d@ethionet.et
Web: www.axumhotels.com

A typical hotel room, but after months on the road, it was divine! Despite the bigger price tag, there was no toilet seat or shower curtain, and every time you took a shower, everything in the bathroom got wet!

US$80.00 for a single room with a double bed.

One of the shock absorber pins is broken, and on a routine examination Wilbur discovered a crack between the mounting for the box body and the chassis – not too surprising considering the roads we have been on. Brian has his share of problems too – brakes, shocks and a leaking water tank. We need to have our second diesel tank welded and repaired, as one tank will never be enough for the long distances between refueling stations. The Kargs have several problems too and to top it all, Lorraine spilt tea on her PC and now it's very sick indeed!

Ingrid Hardman

Breakfast was included in the price and we soon learnt that breakfast in Ethiopia meant eggs with chillies and warm bread! Don't be surprised when you order a boiled egg to see that the size of the egg is not much bigger than a pigeon's!

Across the road from the Axum Hotel is a three-storey building with a coffee shop-cum-restaurant on the top floor. They serve delicious cakes and a good evening meal for a reasonable price. There is also a small supermarket, bookshop and jewellery store where you can purchase one of the many beautiful Ethiopian crosses.

■ Addis Ababa to Woldiya

It is approximately 534 kilometres from Addis Ababa to Woldiya.

From the Axum Hotel, follow the Haile Gebreselassie Road (Route 1), in a northeasterly direction to Debre Berhan, approximately 145 kilometres away. Although the road is tarred, the going is slow due to animals, buses and people. Fuel was available at Debre Berhan.

From here on to Woldiya, via Kombolcha (N11°04.833' E39°44.650') and Dese, the roads were under construction as a result of rain damage from the previous year. Added to that was the 3 000 metre climb up the hills and back down again on the other side. Thunderstorms and the sudden appearance of waterfalls resulted in mud slides and loose stones across the road. Despite all of the above, the dirt roads were in good condition!

Diesel was available at Kombolcha for Birr15.30 per litre. Fuel and banking facilities were available at Dese and Woldiya, which is also the last spot to stock up on necessities before leaving for Lalibela.

Lal Hotel

Tel: (011) 6626586
Cell: 0930034708
E-mail: info@lalhoteltour.com
Web: www.lalhoteltour.com

Situated on the main road, as you enter Woldiya.

Birr500.00 for a room with a double bed and hot water shower. Breakfast was not included. Secure parking.

ETHIOPIA – ROUTE PLANNING

En route to Lalibela we came across several young boys selling bunches of carrots for Birr1.00. Feeling a little peckish, we stopped to buy a bunch. The green tops had been platted, and the carrots scrubbed clean in the cold water of mountain streams. After the first sweet bite, we were hooked. I lost count on the number of carrots we both consumed that day, but I do know that Bugs Bunny would have been proud!

■ Woldiya to Lalibela

It is approximately 180 kilometres from Woldiya to Lalibela.

From Woldiya you will need to head west on the Gondar road to Gashena, otherwise known as Bet Hor (N11°41.303' E38°55.432'). Turn north here to Lalibela, approximately 67 kilometres away. At the T-junction (N11°57.619' E39°00.693') take a right turn and follow the road up to Lalibela. Once at the top, the road will open into the main square. Take a left turn and follow the road down the hill where it will swing to the left and cross over the Jordan River.

Although the roads are in fairly good condition, it will take you several hours to reach Lalibela. The scenery is awesome, the gelada baboons are amazing and the stone cottages **(below)** look like they belong in Ireland. There is a lot to see and photograph. Take your time and revel in its beauty.

Male gelada baboon

ROUTE PLANNING – ETHIOPIA

Panoramic View Hotel

Tel: (033) 3360270
E-mail: info@panoramicviewhotel.com
Web: www.panoramicviewhotel.com

High up on the Lalibela Mountains with breathtaking views of the surrounding Ethiopian highlands and countryside in all directions. The famous churches of Lalibela are only a 10 minute walk away. A single room costs US$45.00 and a double room US$55.00. Breakfast is included.

The Churches of Lalibela

The ticket office is situated in a small parking area, near the Jordan River.

Tickets may be purchased between 06:00 and 12:00, and again between 14:00 and 17:00. The entrance fee is US$50.00 per person and is valid for 5 days.

Licensed guides can usually be found around the ticket office area. The fee charged (Birr600.00 per per person per day) by each individual should be negotiated and agreed upon before setting off.

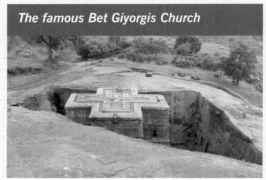

The famous Bet Giyorgis Church

ETHIOPIA – ROUTE PLANNING

All I can say is even if you are not a Christian or even religious, you cannot fail to be blown away by the grandeur and workmanship of this church (Bet Giyorgis).

The floors and steps have been smoothed by the feet of thousands of pilgrims, and the massive doors are carved from olive trees.

Within the hollowed out caves lay the mummified bodies of pilgrims from the 16th and 17th century.

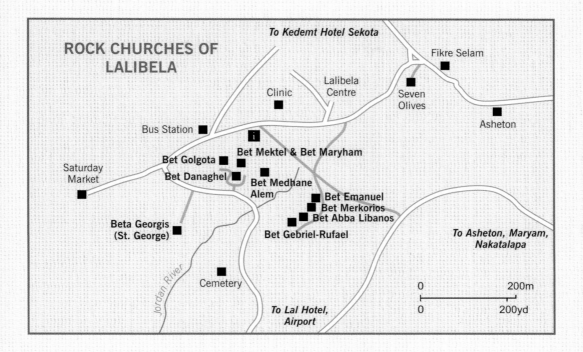

ROCK CHURCHES OF
LALIBELA

To Kedemt Hotel Sekota

Fikre Selam

Clinic

Lalibela
Centre

Seven
Olives

Asheton

Bus Station

Bet Mektel & Bet Maryham

Bet Golgota

Bet Danaghel

Saturday
Market

Bet Medhane
Alem

Bet Emanuel
Bet Merkorios
Bet Abba Libanos

Beta Georgis
(St. George)

Bet Gebriel-Rufael

To Asheton, Maryam,
Nakatalapa

Jordan River

Cemetery

0   200m

0   200yd

To Lal Hotel,
Airport

Take your wallet with you as you will also be required to pay the car guard, make a donation at each church, pay the 'shoe minder' and help the poor!

Photographs may be taken inside the church but the use of a flash is forbidden. The use of a video is permitted, however the fee charged is exorbitant.

You will be required to remove your shoes when entering each church and women must have their head, arms and legs covered.

Lalibela's churches are divided into two clusters, separated by the Jordan River. It took us a day and a half to view four churches in only one cluster.

ROUTE PLANNING – ETHIOPIA

We saw an ancient worn and faded manuscript, written in Ge'ez on paper-thin goat skin and magnificent processional crosses.

Of one thing I am convinced though, these all deserve to be acknowledged as the Eighth Wonder of the Ancient World.

■ Lalibela to Mekelle

It is approximately 342 kilometres from Lalibela to Mekelle.

Proceed back to the main square and take a left turn heading north to the town of Sekota. Although a fairly good gravel road, we ended up with two flat tyres along this stretch! After approximately 100 kilometres, you will come to a junction at which you will need to take a right turn. This dirt road will lead you back to the main north/south road (Route 1), roughly 75 kilometres away.

Once there, take a left turn and head north to Mekelle via Maychew and Korem.

Fuel was available in Maychew.

Mekelle

Mekelle is a fairly large city with all the usual facilities. We arrived in the late afternoon and left the following morning, having spent a wee fortune on tyre repairs, a new tube, a painting of Mary and a Lalibela cross.

Yordanos Hotel

Tel: (034) 4413722
E-mail: info@yordanoshotels.com
Web: www.yordanoshotels.com

Situated in Godena Mizer Road. A single room costs US$44.00, a standard room US$55.00 and a twin room US$71.50.

ROUTE PLANNING – ETHIOPIA

One who plants grapes by the road side, and one who marries a pretty woman, share the same problem.

Ethiopian Proverb

Each church we passed, and there were plenty, had a small collection box for donations on the side of the road **(above right)**. It looked like a 'miniature church' about a metre high. Some are draped in scarves or under ornate umbrellas.

Ingrid Hardman

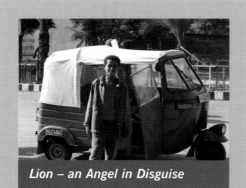

Lion – an Angel in Disguise

Mekelle to Aksum

It is approximately 230 kilometres from Mekelle to Aksum.

Continue heading north along Route 1 to Aksum on a good tar road. As you approach Adigrat, take a left turn at the traffic circle and head for Aksum on a bumpy dirt road.

Banking facilities, supermarket stores and diesel is available in Aksum.

The hundred or so kilometres to Aksum were very different to the previous six days. High sandstone cliffs dominated the area, and the twisty, tight bends in the road must test the truck and bus drivers' nerves. Basins of prickly pears lined the roadsides, and in the distance we could make out the jagged, misshapen mountains that form the outer fringes of the Simien Range.

We arrived in Aksum, a World Heritage Site and the Queen of Sheba's capital in the 10th century! A young boy of no more than 12 years, with an unpronounceable name, latched onto Brian's truck shouting, 'Hello, South Africa! Bafana, Bafana! I will be your guide in Aksum and I will show you a very nice hotel.' He was an absolute gem and obviously very bright and enthusiastic. He organised someone to do a mountain of washing for me and fetched the guys two cold beers and bread rolls. He informed us his nickname was 'Lion' and he would meet us on Monday for a tour of the town!

Ingrid Hardman

Engraving on a Stelae

Aksum

Aksum is a World Heritage Site and one of Ethiopia's main attractions. It is a small, quiet town with all the usual amenities.

There is a lot to see and do here. In one day we visited the Queen of Sheba's bath and palace, the old and new St. Mary of Zion Churches, and the massive granite stelae marking the burial sites of past kings. Unfortunately, the archaeological museum was closed.

Africa Hotel

Tel: (034) 7753700

This hotel is situated on the right-hand side of the main road as you enter Aksum. If you reach the Ezana Garden, where the road splits in two, then you have gone too far. There is good secure parking and the rooms are clean and well maintained.

Birr400.00.00 for a room with a double bed.

EZANA GARDEN – Lying in the garden is the famous stone of the 4th century King Ezana. The stone is of great historical value in that it records honorary titles and military victories achieved by King Ezana, and is written in three ancient scripts – Ge'ez, Sabaean and Greek. It also records the King's conversion to Christianity.

ATTRACTIONS

Church of St. Mary of Zion – Legend has it that the Church is the repository of the Ark of the Covenant, which is said to have been stolen from the temple of Jerusalem by Menelik I, Solomon's own son by the legendary Queen of Sheba. There are two churches in the compound: the old church, which was built by Emperor Fasiladas in 1665, and a new church built in the 1960's by Haile Selassie.

Northern Stelae Field – The numerous monolithic stelae are fashioned out of solid granite. Their mystery lies in that it is not known exactly by whom, and for what purpose, they were fashioned, although they were likely associated with burials of emperors. The biggest monolith (and the largest in the world), measuring over 33m (108 ft) and weighing about 500 tonnes, fell somewhere around the 4th Century AD and now lies in broken fragments on the ground.

Palace of the Queen of Sheba – only the foundations of this palace remain. Although called the Palace of the Queen of Sheba, it actually dates from the 7th century AD, about 1500 years after the time of Queen of Sheba.

Lioness of Gobedra – a stone carving of a lion, a few kilometres out of town in the direction of Shire. It is close to the quarry where the stelae were made.

Clockwise from top left: ancient manuscripts, crowns of past Ethiopian rulers, stelae and the St. Mary of Zion cross

ETHIOPIA – ROUTE PLANNING

DID YOU KNOW?

No satisfactory explanation has been given as to how such a massive block of stone was erected. Axumite tradition has it that it was the work of the mysterious powers of the Ark of the Covenant. The stelae above, is carved with a door and nine windows, that are thought to symbolise the door and nine chambers of King Ezana's Tomb.

■ Aksum to Debark

It is approximately 260 kilometres from Aksum to Debark.

From the Africa Hotel, head towards the Ezana Garden, where the main road (Route 1) splits into two. Follow the road to the right. Once you have passed the Ezana Garden, take a left turn, followed by a right turn and you're back on Route 1, which will now become Route 3. The tar road is in good condition but will eventually become a dirt road with the odd pothole. Continue along Route 3 until you reach Debark.

Debark

There is not much of interest in Debark, but it is here that you will find the Simien Mountains National Park headquarters and booking office. The main road passes through the town and the Simien Park Hotel, easily recognisable, is on the left-hand side of the road and the park headquarters is further up the road on the right-hand side.

On today's journey we saw jigsaw puzzle fields in green and brown, sweeping up to the highlands where daily temperatures range between 11°C and 18°C and where the altitude is between 2,000 and 4,500 metres! Bend after bend we were treated to the sight of the magnificent and jagged Simien Mountains – home of the gelada baboon, walia ibex and the Ethiopian wolf. This truly is the 'Roof of Africa.' Tumbling cascades of water, indigenous forests with wisps of clouds drifting by and our first sight of the gelada baboon. Our radios crackled with static from the approaching storm and then the first ping ping of rain. Within seconds the roads and waterfalls gushed with water. We arrived at the Simien Park Hotel and, my gosh ... all the winter woollies came out. It was freezing.

Ingrid Hardman

ROUTE PLANNING – ETHIOPIA

The majestic Simien Mountains

Simien Mountains National Park

Tel: (058) 1170422
E-mail: info@simienmountains.org
Web: www.simienmountains.org

The best time to visit the park is from December to March, during the dry season. October is also a good time to visit, as the rains have ended and the scenery is at its best with all the wild flowers in bloom. Unfortunately, we arrived in the middle of the rainy season, which meant low cloud cover, mist and wet, slippery conditions. We were advised not to enter the park as there would be very little of the majestic mountains to see.

The entry fee is Birr90.00 per person and camping costs Birr40.00 per person. The presence of a guide is mandatory and insurance against complications is advisable.

Simien Park Hotel

Tel: (058) 1170055/0406
E-mail: senhabtamu@gmail.com
Web: www.simienparkhotel.com

The accommodation here is made up of single rooms with a clean communal shower. There is a small restaurant on site and good security. A single room costs Birr300.00 and a double room Birr400.00. Breakfast is not included.

ETHIOPIA – ROUTE PLANNING

Many Ethiopians, men and women, have crosses tattooed on their foreheads and jawlines, and for some reason the country has more than its share of crippled and blind people.

Ingrid Hardman

■ Debark to Gondar

It is approximately 102 kilometres from Debark to Gondar.

Continue along Route 3 out of Debark, and head for Gondar along a dirt road with a few ruts.

Supermarkets, banking facilities and diesel at Birr15.52 per litre were available in Gondar.

Gondar

Gondar is known as Africa's Camelot with its castles (below) and churches, and is one of the major attractions along this historical route.

The Royal Enclosure, dating as far back as 1640, houses several beautiful castles, a banqueting hall, lion enclosure, bathing pool, stables, and much more.

The entrance fee is US$6.00 per person. The use of a video camera costs US$5.00. The minimum fee for a guide is US$9.00.

As you enter Gondar, continue along the main road, which will eventually lead you past the front entrance gate to the Royal Enclosure, easily identified by its high stone wall.

Michael Hotel

Tel: (058) 1110020
Web: www.michaelhotel.com

This hotel is located in the centre of Gondar at the Italian built piazza, and is within walking distance of the Royal Enclosure.

A single room costs Birr250.00 and Birr300.00 for a twin room.

Debre Berhan Selassie Church

Meaning 'Trinity at the Mount of Light.' One of the most beautiful churches in Ethiopia, and well known for its ceiling decorated with the faces of 80 Ethiopian cherubs. Apparently, this church was built with care and attention to house the Ark of the Covenant. The perimeter wall has 12 round towers, representing the 12 apostles; the gateway is the 13th tower and represents Christ. The entrance fee is Birr25.00 per person.

Photographs of this amazing church can be seen overleaf.

The tail of a lion is carved on the key-stone of the arch, in the wall to the west of the church, signifying the omnipresence of Christ

The perimeter wall has twelve round towers representing the twelve apostles

ETHIOPIA – ROUTE PLANNING

The Father, the Son and the Holy Spirit

On the top of the roof are seven niches supporting a seven pronged medallion, with an ostrich egg on each prong. Seven signifies the seven days of creation and the eggs represent the power of the creative spirit

One of the 80 Ethiopian cherubs that adorn the roof and walls of the Debre Berhan Selassie Church

■ Gondar to Addis Ababa

It is approximately 770 kilometres from Gondar to Addis Ababa.

From the Royal Enclosure, follow the road (Route 3) back into town. At the first traffic circle, take a left turn and head for Bahir Dar on Route 3. This is a good tar road with fuel available en route.

We had intended to visit Lake Tana and the Blue Nile Falls, but broke a rear-side shaft and thought it sensible to stick to the main road and head back to Addis Ababa. Halfway there, the radiator hose popped, taking over an hour to fix! To top it all, we missed the campsite in the dark and had to push on to Addis Ababa. This trip is not advisable at night due to the high number of hyenas on the road, unmarked parked vehicles on the verge, and oncoming traffic with either no lights or only one light on bright.

After several days in Addis Ababa, we sadly headed south, starting the long trip back home; with amazing memories and a thousand-odd photographs of a truly awesome trip.

Would we do it again? You bet!

ETHIOPIA – ROUTE PLANNING

Cherengani Hills, Kenya

■ With Hindsight

- Pack less. If you have a good relationship with your travelling companions and will be together for the duration of the trip, share equipment and spares to lighten the load and avoid duplication.

- Lock everything on the outside of your vehicle.

- Plan the inside of the vehicle carefully. If it becomes an effort to retrieve anything, rethink the layout.

- I recommend a trial run before the trip to iron out any problems.

- An awning with one or more light-duty sides is a necessity when dealing with excessive wind and rain.

- When in use, protect the gas stove from wind.

- Keep fruit and vegetables in a grass basket or box to help prevent damage en route.

- Carry a rimless spare tyre to lighten the load.

- Stainless steel, used to make water tanks, invariably springs a leak along the join points. Rather use heavy-duty plastic.

- Long-range fuel tanks should be able to cover a minimum distance of a 1 000 kilometres.

- A Visa card gives you better access to your money. We used a Mastercard and had to borrow money on several occasions when the ATM would not accept it.

- All vehicles in the convoy must be connected via two-way radio.

- We carried US$7 000.00 in emergency funds. It was used to change money at the border post until we could get to the nearest ATM or bank.

- Hiring a boat in Africa is a costly experience. We carried a rubber duck, seating four people. With hindsight, we would change the engine size to 15 horsepower.

- Cable bush deflectors are not necessary.

- We used the underside of the opened end of the rooftop tent to dry towels and underwear overnight.

- A comprehensive toolkit is necessary. We used a good one from Mastercraft.

- Store charcoal in a canvas bag to stop the black dust making a mess.

- A rollbar can be life-saving.

- Most vehicle alarms are not waterproof. This could become a problem down the road. Try and protect the unit with a plastic bag and learn how to disconnect the alarm in case you run into trouble.

- Read a book on Ethiopia – it's a fascinating place.

- Slow down – you're on holiday and may never pass this way again. Spend more time in places of greater interest.

- If it moves, take a photograph!

- Visit the local markets. They are colourful and full of interesting people and food.

- Set out early in the morning, when the day is cool and the road traffic is light.

- Think carefully before crossing over to Europe and shipping your vehicle back. Europe is expensive and like our unfortunate friends, you may have your vehicle broken into on board the ship.

- Store your computer in a dust-proof padded case.

- Take some business cards for valuable contacts you may meet along the way.

- Keep a daily diary on your computer and save it regularly on a flash drive. You can use the flash drive for a quick letter home when you find an Internet café.

- Purchase a couple of sarongs and have them made into skirts. They are cool to wear, wash easily, dry overnight and do not need to be ironed.

- For clothing repairs, take a tube of 'Sew Simple' from Bostik.

- A plastic potty is a necessity at night, especially when in the company of wild animals!

- Pack biscuits into tins and seal the lid with greaseproof paper.

- Purchase small disposable packets of salad dressing to avoid wastage.

- Cook extra at dinner time, for lunch the following day.

- Purchase a kettle with a folding handle.

> It always seems impossible until its done.
>
> – *Nelson Mandela*

Payback!!!

INDEX

A

Abuna Aregawi 165
Abuna Samuel............................165
Addis Ababa 158, 177, 178, 180, 194
Adigrat 158, 186
Africa Hotel...............................187
Airlines 48, 63, 72, 96, 120, 160
Aksum .158, 159, 186, 187, 188, 189
Amabere Caves..................105, 106
An African Blessing 3
Arba Minch 158, 170, 172
Arba Minch Shecha............170, 171
Arba Minch Sikela......170, 171, 172
Arusha..........70, 71, 89, 90, 91, 93
Arusha National Park 90
Athi River 118
Automobile Association....48, 63, 72, 96, 120
Axum Hotel 178, 179, 180

B

Bahir Dar 158, 194
Bale Mountains National Par 158, 159, 174, 175, 176, 177
Bangweulu Wetland ..46, 47, 56, 57, 58
Bekele Molla Hotel.............166, 177
Bet Giyorgis 183
Bet Hor 181
Blue Nile Falls...........................194
Border Crossing 48, 64, 72, 96, 121, 161
Bujagali Falls 99, 114
Bush Recipes 28

C

Cab Requirements 17
Carnet de Passage 12, 13
Chalbi Desert 155
Chalinze 85
Chencha 171, 172
Cherangani Hills 118, 132, 134
Chilumba 62, 66, 67, 68
Chimpanzees...............95, 107, 108
Chitimba 67
Chitipa Border Post 46, 66

Chorlim Wildlife Sanctuary 116, 131, 132

Choosing a Campsite.....................6
Church Etiquette........................161
Climate.....48, 64, 73, 96, 121, 161
Clothing and Toiletries.................32
Coffee Tree Campsite 88
Comesa Yellow Card 13
Compiling an Itinerary 8
Crying Stone of Ilesi 129

D

Dar es Salaam 70, 72, 73, 74, 75, 76, 82, 83, 84, 85, 86
David Livingstone 77
Debark 158, 189, 191
Debre Berhan 158, 180
Debre Berhan Selassie Church..191–193
Debre Damo Hotel 178
Debre Markos............................158
Debre Zeyit 178
Dese 180
Diani Beach 118, 141, 142, 143
Diani Campsite and Cottages.......142
Dinsho 158, 174
Dinsho Lodge 175, 177
Diplomatic Missions ..48, 64, 73, 96, 121, 161
Distant Relatives Eco Lodge and Backpackers...........................144
Documentation 12
Dorze 171

E

Eden Rock Resort 114
Eldoret 118
Electricity..49, 64, 73, 97, 121, 162
Elsamere Conservation Centre 127
Enangiperi 136
Entebbe 94, 101
Entebbe Airport 95, 101
Equipment...................................23
Ethiopia....................................158
Ethiopian Saints 164, 165
Ethiopian Wolf 176
Eureka Camp 53, 54
Explorers Camp 99, 100
Ezana Garden............................187

F

Fiche..158
Fisherman's Camp 126
Forest Inn 54, 55
Fort Portal..........94, 105, 106, 109
Fun Safaris 92

G

Garissa 118, 147, 148
Garsen......................118, 146, 147
Gashena 181
Gede Ruins 118, 119, 145
Gelada Baboons 181
German Boma..............................78
Gilgil 127
Gobe 174
Gondar 158, 159, 181, 191, 194
Government Guest House 148
Grocery List 26

H

Harenna Forest..................158, 176
Hells Gate National Park............127
Hoima 94, 105, 106
Hot Springs...............................173

I

Ibanda 110
Iganga 115
Ikwiri 82
Irente Viewpoint 86
Iringa 70
Isanga Bay Lodge 47, 60, 61
Isoka 46
Isiolo 118, 149, 150
Itezhi-Tezhi Dam 53

J

Jinja.............94, 99, 101,114, 115
Jinka...167

K

Kabernet...................................134
Kabula Lodge 46, 47, 51, 52
Kafue National Park ...46, 51, 52, 53
Kalambo Falls 46, 47, 60, 61
Kakamega.........118, 122, 127, 129
Kakamega Forest National Park ..118, 119, 127, 130, 131

Kampala ..94, 95, 101, 102, 112, 114
Kanyanchu Camp 108
Kapchorwa..................94, 115, 116
Kapiri Mposhi..................46, 54, 55
Kapishya Hot Springs 47, 58, 59
Kapsabet 127
Karonga...................62, 66, 68, 69
Kasama..............................46, 59
Kasanka National Park 46, 55, 56
Kasese...............94, 109, 110, 111
Kasumulu Border Post............70, 76
Katima Mulilo 46
Kazungula Border Post 46, 51
Kazungula Ferry....................46, 49
Kenya 118
Key Afar 167
Kibale Forest National Park....94, 95,
    106, 109
Kigamboni Pontoon.....................83
Kilifi 143, 144
Kilwa Dreams..............................80
Kilwa Kisiwani...........70, 71, 80, 81
Kilwa Masoko.................70, 80, 82
Kinango...................................142
Kipepeo Beach Village.................83
Kitale 118, 134
Kitchen Utensils 25
Kokot Hotel................................166
Kombolcha 180
Konso......................158, 167, 170
Korem 185
Korogwe 86
Kundilila Falls 55, 56
Kwale...............................142

L

Lake Abaya...............................170
Lake Albert 94, 110
Lake Bogoria 118, 132, 133, 134,
    135, 136
Lake Chala..................................88
Lake Chamo..............................170
Lake Edward 94, 111, 112
Lake Elmenteita.................127, 128
Lake George................................94
Lake Magadi 118, 119, 140, 141
Lake Malawi........62, 63, 66, 67, 70
Lake Naivasha...118, 124, 126, 127
Lake Tana........................158, 194
Lake Tanganyika..46, 47, 60, 61, 70

Lake Turkana ...118, 119, 151, 152,
    153, 154
Lake Victoria 70, 94, 118, 119
Lal Hotel 180
Lalibela....158, 159, 173, 178, 180,
    181, 182, 183, 185
Lamu Island 118, 119, 146, 147
Lawns Hotel................................87
Lindi 77
Livingstone 46, 52
Livingstonia 62, 67
Loyangalani.......118, 152, 154, 155
Luangwa National Park 46
Lusaka 46, 47, 52, 53, 54
Lushoto 70, 71, 86, 87, 88
Luwero 94

M

Maasai 90
Makambako 70, 77
Malaba Border Post 118, 131
Malawi................................61, 62
Malindi............................118, 146
Maralal 118, 151, 152
Marangu..............................88, 89
Marigat.............................118, 134
Marsabit..........................118, 155
Marsabit National Park 118, 155,
    156
Masai Mara National
    Reserve........118, 119, 136, 137,
    139, 140
Masaka 94
Masasi 70, 77
Masindi 94, 102
Maychew 158, 185
Mbala....................46, 59, 60, 61
Mbale..............................94, 115
Mbalizi 77
Mbarara 94, 112
Mbeya.........................70, 76, 77
Medical..19, 49, 64, 74, 97, 122, 162
Mekelle.............................185–186
Meserani Snake Park..71, 91, 92, 93
Mikindani 70, 71, 77, 78, 79
Mkushi...........................46, 55
Mnarani Ruins........................144
Mojo 158, 159, 178
Mokowe 146, 147
Mombasa.................118, 141, 143

Mombo 86, 88
Money 49, 65, 74, 97, 122, 162
Mongu..................46, 51, 52, 53
Mora Heights Hotel 170
Morogoro....................................70
Moshi........................70, 89, 90
Moyale 155, 156, 158, 159, 166,
    167
Moyale Border Post...118, 156, 158,
    166
Mpika 46, 56, 58
Mpulungu 46, 59, 60
Msimbati Peninsula 71
Mt. Elgon............94, 116, 118, 131
Mt Kenya......................118, 149
Mt Kilimanjaro 70, 88
Mt Meru 90
Mtwara........................70, 71, 79
Mubuku......................................109
Muheza 86
Murchison Falls National Park......94,
    95, 102, 103, 104, 105
Mwanga 88
Mweya 111

N

Nairobi 118, 119, 124, 125, 126,
    140, 141
Naivasha 118, 126, 136
Nakasongola 94, 102
Nakuru 118, 127
Namanga Border Post ...70, 93, 118,
    124
Nanyuki...........................118, 149
Naro Moru 118, 148, 149
Naro Moru River Lodge..............149
Narok......................118, 136, 140
Nechisar National Park.......158, 170
New Kalala Camp.........................53
Ngonye Falls 46, 52
Ngorongoro Crater10, 70, 71, 91, 92
Niamkolo Church..................46, 60
Njombe 77
Njoro 136
Nkupi Lodge 59, 60
North Horr 118, 155
Nyakalengija 110
Nyika National Park 62, 67
Njoro 136
Nungwi 84

O

Ol Donyo Sabuk National Park.....149
Oloika Sange Beach Bumgalows....86
Olorgasailie Prehistoric Site.........140
Omo Valley 158, 159, 167, 170
Omorate 167
Our Journey at a Glance 38

P

Palm Shade Camp 154
Pangani...........................70, 71, 86
Panoramic View Hotel 182
Pemba Island 70, 75
Planning on the Homefront 34
Public Holidays..49, 65, 74, 97, 122, 162
Putsi Fly..................................108

Q

Queen Elizabeth National
    Park 94, 110–112

R

Red Chilli Hideaway..................102
Red Chilli Restcamp..................105
Rovuma Bay 70
Rufiji River............................71, 82
Rules of the Road 7, 49, 65, 74, 97, 122, 162
Ruvula 79, 80
Ruvula Safaris............................79
Ruvula Village 71
Ruwenzori Mountains National
    Park 94, 109–111

S

Safari Ants 108
Samburu 142
Samburu National Reserve.118, 119, 149, 150
Same 88
Sangilo Lodge.............................66
Satellite Phone 9
Segera..........................70, 85, 86
Sekota......................................185
Serengeti National
    Park 70, 71, 91, 92, 136, 139
Serenje....................46, 47, 55, 56
Service Telephone Numbers and Area
    Codes ...50, 65, 74, 98, 122, 163
Shashemene 158, 172, 173, 174, 177

Shimba Hills National Reserve....118, 143
Shimoni Village 143
Shiwa Ngandu...........46, 47, 58, 59
Shoebill Island.............................57
Shoebill Stork 57, 101, 103, 117
Sigor 118, 134
Simien Mountains National
    Park 158, 189, 190
Simien Park Hotel 189, 190
Sipi Falls 95, 115, 116
Smart Card 123
Sodo 158, 172, 173
Songea 70, 71, 77
Songwe Border Post.........62, 68, 70
South Horr..................118, 151
Speke Memorial..........................99
Stone Town.................................84
Suam Border Post ..94, 116, 118, 131
Subira House 147

T

Tanga 70, 85–86
Taxis...163
Tanzania 70
Ten Degrees South.......................78
The Royal Enclosure...................191
The Slipway 75
Thika 118, 148, 149
Tororo Border Post ..94, 99, 115, 116
Tot...................................118, 134
Tour Holiday Inn.........................110
Travel Companions 6
Trinity Guest House.....................83
Tunduma.....................................47
Tunduma Border Post.......46, 47, 61, 70–71
Tunduru 70, 77, 79
Twilight Guest House 115, 116

U

Uganda 94
Uganda Wildlife Education Centre ...95, 101
Utengule Coffee Lodge..................76

V

Vehicle Assistance 50, 65, 75, 98, 123, 163
Vehicle Insurance 13
Vehicle Requirements...................14

Victoria Nile...95, 100, 103, 104, 114
Visa 48, 64, 72, 96, 121, 161
Voi..118

W

Wamba 118, 150, 151
Watamu....118, 143, 144, 145, 146
Websites and Books for Additional
    Information...50, 65, 76, 99, 123, 163
Webuye.....................................131
Weyto 167
Wildebeest Eco Camp 125
With Hindsight 197, 198
Woldiya 158, 180, 181
Wondo Genet ...158, 159, 172, 173, 174
Wondo Genet Resort Hotel..........173

Y

Yabelo................................158, 167
Yordanos Hotel.........................185

Z

Zambia......................................46
Zanzibar Ferry 73, 83, 84
Zanzibar Island...............70, 71, 84
Zambezi River 51
Zanzibar 71, 75, 84, 86
Ziway.................................177, 178